前言 *PREFACE*

英国思想家培根说过：阅读使人深刻。阅读的真正目的是获取信息，开拓视野和陶冶情操。从语言学习的角度来说，学习语言若没有大量阅读就如隔靴搔痒，因为阅读中的语言是最丰富、最灵活、最具表现力、最符合生活情景的，同时读物中的情节、故事引人入胜，进而能充分调动读者的阅读兴趣，培养读者的文学修养，至此，语言的学习水到渠成。

"麦格希中英双语阅读文库"在世界范围内选材，涉及科普、社会文化、文学名著、传奇故事、成长励志等多个系列，充分满足英语学习者课外阅读之所需，在阅读中学习英语、提高能力。

◎难度适中

本套图书充分照顾读者的英语学习阶段和水平，从读者的阅读兴趣出发，以难易适中的英语语言为立足点，选材精心、编排合理。

◎精品荟萃

本套图书注重经典阅读与实用阅读并举。既包含国内外脍炙人口、耳熟能详的美文，又包含科普、人文、故事、励志类等多学科的精彩文章。

◎功能实用

本套图书充分体现了双语阅读的功能和优势，充分考虑到读者课外阅读的方便，超出核心词表的词汇均出现在使其意义明显的语境之中，并标注释义。

鉴于编者水平有限，凡不周之处，谬误之处，皆欢迎批评教正。

我们真心地希望本套图书承载的文化知识和英语阅读的策略对提高读者的英语著作欣赏水平和英语运用能力有所裨益。

丛书编委会

社会文化系列

麦格希 中英双语阅读文库

乔治·华盛顿：美国国父

社会生活馆 第1辑

麦格希中英双语阅读文库编委会●编

吉林出版集团股份有限公司

图书在版编目（CIP）数据

社会生活馆.第1辑,乔治·华盛顿：美国国父 /
美国麦格劳-希尔教育集团主编；王丹丹等译；麦格希
中英双语阅读文库编委会编. -- 2版. -- 长春：吉林出
版集团股份有限公司, 2018.3
（麦格希中英双语阅读文库）
书名原文: Timed Readings Plus in Social Studies Book 1
ISBN 978-7-5581-4789-0

Ⅰ.①社… Ⅱ.①美… ②王… ③麦… Ⅲ.①英语—
汉语—对照读物②社会科学—通俗读物 Ⅳ.
①H319.4：C

中国版本图书馆CIP数据核字(2018)第046399号

社会生活馆　第1辑　乔治·华盛顿：美国国父

编：麦格希中英双语阅读文库编委会
插　　画：齐　航　李延霞
责任编辑：王芳芳　孟程程
封面设计：冯冯翼
开　　本：660mm×960mm　1/16
字　　数：225千字
印　　张：10
版　　次：2018年3月第2版
印　　次：2018年3月第1次印刷

出　　版：吉林出版集团股份有限公司
发　　行：吉林出版集团外语教育有限公司
地　　址：长春市泰来街1825号
　　　　　邮编：130011
电　　话：总编办：0431-86012683
　　　　　发行部：0431-86012767　0431-86012826(Fax)
印　　刷：香河利华文化发展有限公司

ISBN 978-7-5581-4789-0　　定价：29.90元

Contents

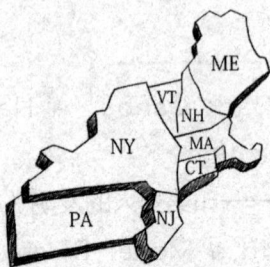

1

George Washington: The Father of Our Country

George Washington was the first *president* of the United States. He is known as the Father of Our Country. He is called this because so much of his life was spent in service to America.

Washington was born in Virginia in 1732. He grew to be a tall, strong boy. As a teen, his older brother, Lawrence, helped him

乔治·华盛顿：美国国父

乔治·华盛顿，美国第一任总统，以国父著称。他之所以被称之为国父正是因为他几乎把一生都献给了自己的祖国。

华盛顿1732年出生于弗吉尼亚州。他个子很高，身体强壮。少年时期他就跟随哥哥劳伦斯学习土地测量。17岁时，他成为了县土地测量员。

---

president *n.* 总统；国家主席

learn to survey land. When he was 17, he became county surveyor. When Lawrence died, George took over his job in the *militia*. George was given the rank of major. He had to gather and inspect the troops. Washington was a strong leader, so he was put in charge of all of Virginia's troops. For three years, he defended Virginia's west border. He also was a leader in the French and Indian War.

In 1759 he returned home to his farm, Mount Vernon. He set up a *mill* and an *ironworks*. He married a widow, Martha Custis. He also served in state government. He opposed many British policies. One of these policies was the Stamp Act. This was a British law that taxed the colonies without their *consent*. Washington thought that Britain's rule was not good for the colonies. He felt that America should govern itself.

劳伦斯去世后，华盛顿接替了他在民兵组织的职位，授少校军衔。华盛顿征集并管理军队，因其出色的领导才能，后来受命负责指挥整个弗吉尼亚军队。华盛顿保卫了弗吉尼亚的西部边界整整三年。同时，华盛顿也是对法国和印度战争中的指挥官。

1759年，华盛顿重返家乡，回到他的农场——弗农山庄。他经营了一家磨坊和一家钢铁厂，并与寡妇玛莎·卡斯蒂斯结为连理。同时，他在州政府任职，并对很多英国政策持反对意见，印花税法就是其中之一。印花税法案是英国未经北美殖民地同意而强行向其征税的法律。华盛顿认为英国统治对殖民地的发展不利，而且美国应该自治。

---

militia *n.* 民兵组织；国民卫队   mill *n.* 磨坊

ironworks *n.* 钢铁厂   consent *n.* 准许；同意

When the Revolutionary War broke out in 1775, Washington was made commander in chief of the Continental Army. His troops had had no training. He had few supplies. His plan was to have patience and to *harass* the British at every chance. In battle, he would fall back at first. Then he would launch a surprise *strike*. After six years, he forced the British to give up.

People felt that Washington was a hero. They wanted him to be the first president. Some even wanted to make him king. He did not want to be president. He wanted to go home. He wanted to spend the rest of his life working on his farm. However, Washington knew that the first president would *pave the way* for the future. He wanted to help form the nation he had served so well. So in 1789, he took the *oath* of office.

　　1775年，独立战争爆发，华盛顿被任命为大陆军总司令。他的军队未经训练，而且供给匮乏。华盛顿的战术是耐心等待，抓住一切机会打击英国军队。战斗中，他会先撤退，然后出其不意地反击。六年后，英国被迫投降。

　　华盛顿是美国人心中的英雄，他们想让华盛顿成为首任总统，一些人甚至想让华盛顿成为国王。华盛顿不想当总统，他想回家，他想回到他的农场，余生都在那里度过。但是，华盛顿明白首任总统要为国家未来开辟道路，他希望能为自己一直尽职尽忠的祖国的建国事业做出贡献。因此，1789年，华盛顿宣誓就职。

---

harass *v.* 侵扰；不断攻击　　　　　　　strike *n.* 军事进攻；袭击
pave the way 铺路　　　　　　　　　　　oath *n.* 宣誓；誓言

Washington served as president for eight years. During that time, France was *at war with* Britain. Washington kept the United States out of war. He knew the country needed time to grow strong. After eight years in office, he went back to Mount Vernon and farmed until he died.

　　华盛顿担任了八年总统。他任职期间，正值英法两国交战。华盛顿使美国远离了这场战争，因为他很清楚美国需要时间来发展壮大。八年任职期满后，华盛顿回到了弗农山庄，务农直至生命的最后。

---

at war with　和……作战；交战

2

Mount Vernon

Mount Vernon is the *magnificent* home of George Washington. It stands on a hill in Virginia. The house, which is made of wood, is three stories tall. It was built by George's older brother, Lawrence. It was passed on to George by Lawrence's *widow*. At that time, the house had two floors and seven rooms. It was on

---

弗农山庄

弗农山庄建筑宏伟，是乔治·华盛顿的故居。它坐落于弗吉尼亚州的一座小山上，木质结构，共三层。弗农山庄由华盛顿的哥哥劳伦斯修建，劳伦斯的遗孀将其传给华盛顿。修建时，山庄分上下两层，共有七个房间，占地2 000英亩。华盛顿加盖了第三层并添置了家

---

magnificent *adj.* 壮丽的；宏伟的   widow *n.* 寡妇；遗孀

2,000 *acres* of land. Washington built a third floor and added new furnishings. After he married Martha Custis, she and her two children moved to Mount Vernon. She and George added north and south *wings* to the house.

The whole time Washington lived at Mount Vernon, he worked to make it a grand home. The two-story porch on the front of the mansion is his design. He built a *cupola* (small domed structure) above the roof. From there, one can see the Potomac River. On top of the cupola, he placed a *weathervane*. It is called the Dove of Peace. He rebuilt the gardens and lanes. He increased the size of the estate to 8,000 acres. More than 300 enslaved persons worked the plantation. Washington freed many of them when he died. Now the estate is owned by the Mount Vernon Ladies' Association. They keep the home much as it was in Washington's time.

具。华盛顿和玛莎·卡斯蒂斯结婚后，她和她的两个孩子搬到了弗农山庄。玛莎·卡斯蒂斯和华盛顿一起增建了山庄南北两面的厢房。

在弗农山庄的日子里，华盛顿一直都在努力使山庄变得更加宏伟：他亲自设计了宅邸前面两层高的门廊；在屋顶上建了穹顶天花板（小圆顶结构），在那里波多马克河尽收眼底；他还在穹顶的顶部安了一个称为和平鸽的风向标；他重建了花园，重修了小路；把山庄扩大到了8 000英亩，300多个奴隶在种植园劳作。华盛顿去世时，给其中的许多奴隶恢复了自由身。现在，弗农山庄归弗农山庄妇女会所有，一直保持着与华盛顿生前差不多的样子。

---

acre *n.* 英亩

cupola *n.* 圆屋顶；穹顶

wing *n.* 耳房；厢房

weathervane *n.* 风向标；风标

3

The Birch Bark Canoe: A Native American Invention

Long ago traveling through the thick forests of North America was a problem. There were no roads. However, there were chains of lakes, rivers, and streams. On the banks of these waterways grew pine, *spruce*, *cedar*, and *birch* trees. Birch trees have white or gray *bark* that peels off in sheets. The ancient Native

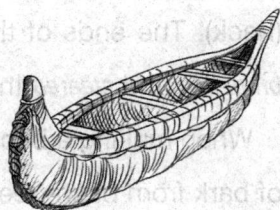

桦树皮独木舟——印第安人的发明

很久以前，在北美茂密的森林里穿行是很困难的事情。那里没有路，却有很多湖泊、河流和小溪。沿岸生长着松树、云杉、雪松和桦树。桦树皮呈白色或灰色，可以成张地剥下来。古代印第安人学会

---

spruce *n.* 云杉　　　　　　　　　　　　　　cedar *n.* 雪松
birch *n.* 桦树　　　　　　　　　　　　　　　bark *n.* 树皮

American peoples learned how to use these trees to build boats. They did not build just any boats—they built birch bark canoes.

Rapids are places where water moves at great speed because a river drops. Rapids are a problem for boats. While going over rapids, a boat can be smashed if it hits the rocks. But a canoe is small and light. A person can carry, or *portage*, a canoe around rapids or from one stream to another.

A canoe is a narrow boat with curved sides. The sides are widest in the middle. They come together at the bow (front) and at the stern (back). The ends of the canoe have a rounded shape. Canoes are *propelled* and *steered* through the water with paddles.

When making a birch bark canoe, Native Americans peeled sheets of bark from birch trees. They then laid the sheets out on a flat piece of ground. The *gunwales* (upper edges) of the canoe were made of wood that was bent to the shape of the canoe. The gunwale frame

---

了如何用这些树木造船，但并不是各种船只他们都制造——他们造的是桦树皮独木舟。

急流是指河流有落差时水流疾速流动的地方。急流是船只的大难题。如果穿越急流时撞上岩石，船只就会撞毁。但独木舟体积小、重量轻，这样在急流附近或者溪流与溪流之间，人们可以把它拿起来或者搬过去。

独木舟很窄，两侧微弯曲，中间最宽，两端呈圆形，两侧在船头和船尾合到一起，船桨起到助力和操纵船的作用。

美国的土著人在制造独木舟时把桦树皮一张张地从桦树上剥下来，然后把桦树皮放在平地上。他们按独木舟的形状把木头折弯做成木制的舷缘

---

portage *v.* 转到陆上运输
steer *v.* 驾驶；操纵

propel *v.* 驱动；推动
gunwale *n.* 舷缘；船舷的上缘

was laid on top of the bark. The edges of the bark were wrapped around the gunwales. Next the birch bark was weighed down with rocks. Then the builders drove wooden *stakes* into the ground around the gunwales. The stakes helped to shape the canoe as it was being built. Then the gunwales were raised to the correct height and held in place.

The *seams* of the bark were sewn together with spruce root. The builders used pine gum, spruce *resin* (sap), and animal fat to make the seams *watertight*. They lined the inside of the canoe with thin sheets of cedar. The lining was held in place by ribs of cedar. The builders cut these ribs and bent them to the shape of the canoe.

When the canoe was finished, an animal was sometimes carved on the outside. Often this was a symbol of the tribe. It took two people—usually a man and a woman—two weeks to build a birch bark canoe.

（上缘），把舷缘框放到桦树皮上，用桦树皮包起来，再用石头把桦树皮压住。随后，造船者在舷缘周围的地里打进一些木桩，这些木桩在造船过程中用来帮助独木舟定型。然后，把弄好的舷抬到合适的高度放好。

造船者用云杉根把桦树皮的边缘缝到一起，用松脂、云杉树脂以及动物脂肪对树皮边缘的接缝进行防水处理。独木舟的里面铺一层薄薄的雪松，用雪松条固定好。造船者砍下雪松条后把它们弯成独木舟的形状。

独木舟造好后，有时船的外面会刻上动物的图案，这些图案通常是部落的象征。造一艘独木舟需要花费两个人（通常是一个男人和一个女人）两周的时间。

---

stake *n.* 桩

resin *n.* 树脂

seam *n.* 接缝；缝隙

watertight *adj.* 不透水的；防水的

4

How to Build a Model Birch Bark Canoe

To build a model of a birch bark canoe, first gather the materials. *Peel off* a length of birch bark from a birch *log* or dead birch tree. Do not peel bark from a live birch tree. If birch bark is not available from a dead tree, use paper. A piece of typing paper or a brown bag will work. A pair of scissors and white glue are needed too.

如何制作桦树皮独木舟模型

制作桦树皮独木舟模型，首先要收集材料。从桦树木材或死桦树上剥下一段桦树皮。不要从活桦树上剥桦树皮。如果在死桦树上找不到可用的桦树皮，就用纸替代。一张打印纸或一个牛皮纸袋就可以了。另外还需要一把剪刀和白胶。

peel off 剥落；去皮　　　　　　　　　　　　　　log *n.* 原木；木材

Step one: Use the scissors to cut a three-inch by five-inch strip of bark or paper.

Step two: Cut the *lengthwise* ends of the bark or paper to make a V. The V should be about one-half inch deep.

Step three: Fold the bark or paper in half, lengthwise.

Step four: *Overlap* the two edges made from cutting the V at each end. Place them so that the top edges are *even* with each other. This is the top edge of the canoe.

Step five: Glue the edges together with white glue. Hold them securely in place so they don't move until the glue dries.

Step six: If using birch bark, try the model canoe out in a sink or a bowl of water. The model will float. A paper model may float for a little while.

Remember, always make sure to ask an adult to help when using scissors.

第一步：用剪刀从桦树皮或纸上剪下五英寸长，三英寸宽的长条。

第二步：在桦树皮或纸的纵长两端各剪一个V型口，V型的深度大约是一英寸半。

第三步：把桦树皮或纸纵向对折。

第四步：把V型两侧的边缘重叠，固定时使V型的边缘对齐，这是独木舟的上缘。

第五步：用白胶把边缘粘上，然后放好，保持不动，直到胶水干透。

第六步：桦树皮做的独木舟模型，可以放在水槽里或一碗水里试一下，模型能浮在水上。纸做的模型则可能只漂浮一小会儿。

要记住：使用剪刀的时候应有大人陪护。

---

lengthwise *adv.* 纵向地
even *adj.* 相等的；均等的

overlap *v.* 重叠；交叠

5

Making Coins at the U.S. Mint

The main purpose of the U.S. Mint is to make coins for use in business and trade. But the *mint* also makes special coins. Some of these are *uncirculated* coin sets, *proof sets*, and *commemorative* coins. Uncirculated coins are coins that have not been used. Proof sets are sets of coins that have been polished and sealed in plastic.

美国铸币局铸造的硬币

美国铸币局的主要任务是铸造在商业和贸易中所使用的硬币，但是铸币局也铸造特殊的硬币：一些非流通硬币套币、精制套币和纪念币。非流通硬币指那些未使用过的硬币；精制套币是指经过抛光并塑封起来的成套硬币；纪念币用来纪念美国的历史和文化。人们购买纪念币的部分钱款投入到有益于社会的事业中。这些特殊的硬币可以用于流

mint *n.* 铸币厂　　　　　　　uncirculated *adj.* 未流通的
proof set 精制套币　　　　　　commemorative *adj.* 纪念的

Commemorative coins honor American history and culture. Part of the money people use to buy commemorative coins goes to good causes. All these special coins can be spent. But they are made to be collected.

Coins are made at four mints. These are in Philadelphia, Pennsylvania; Denver, Colorado; San Francisco, California; and West Point, New York. Each of these mints makes special coins. The Philadelphia and Denver mints also make coins for circulation.

The mints make six kinds of regular coins. They are the *penny*, *nickel*, *dime*, quarter, half-dollar, and dollar coins. Most coins have portraits on one side. The portraits are usually of U.S. presidents. Some of the dollar coins have portraits of famous American women. State quarters—one for each of the 50 states—are now being made. Each state quarter honors one state.

通，但其铸造的目的主要用于收藏。

　　美国有四个铸币局可以铸造硬币，分别是宾夕法尼亚州费城铸币局、科罗拉多州的丹佛铸币局、加利福尼亚州的旧金山铸币局以及纽约州的西点铸币局。这些铸币局都能铸造特殊的硬币。费城和丹佛铸币局也铸造流通的硬币。

　　铸币局铸造的常用硬币有六种，分别是一美分、五美分、十美分、二十五美分、五十美分和一美元。大部分硬币一面是人物头像，通常都是美国总统的头像，还有一些是著名的美国女性的头像。现在，美国的五十个州都发行代表本州的州二十五美分硬币。

---

penny *n.* 一分钱　　　　　　　　　　　　　　　　　nickel *n.* 五分镍币
dime *n.* 十分硬币；十分钱

The mints make coins from blanks, which are called *planchets*. A blank is a metal circle, the right size and thickness for the coin. The mints buy blanks to make pennies, but they make their own nickel blanks. Penny and nickel blanks are made by melting metals together to make an *alloy*. (An alloy is a mixture of two or more metals.) The liquid alloy is then poured into *molds*. The molds shape the metal into blocks, called *ingots*. Coin makers roll the ingots into strips. Then they cut blanks from the strips. Dimes, quarters, half-dollars, and dollars have copper cores. An alloy covers this core. By looking at the edge of the coin, the core can be seen. The mint makes blanks for these coins from metal strips.

To make coins from blanks, workers first soften and clean the blanks. They then roll the edges to make them thicker. Finally the designs are stamped on each side. Dimes, quarters, half-dollars,

---

硬币由硬币坯，即空白硬币制成。硬币坯是圆形的金属物，大小、薄厚和硬币相同。铸币局购买硬币坯铸造一美分硬币，但是自己生产五美分硬币的金属板。一美分和五美分硬币的硬币坯由几种金属熔化后形成的合金制作。（合金通常是两到三种金属的混合物。）制成的液体合金随后倒到模具里。模具把合金定型成模块，这些模块也叫铸块。硬币制造者把这些铸块卷成条状物，然后从条状物上切下硬币坯。十美分、二十五美分、五十美分和一美元硬币的中心部分由铜制成，外面由合金包起来。从硬币的边缘就能看到硬币的中心部分。这些硬币的硬币坯由铸币局用金属条制成。

　　要把硬币坯制成硬币，工人首先要软化并清洁硬币坯，然后转动它

---

planchet *n.* 硬币坯；造币用金属板
mold *n.* 模子

alloy *n.* 合金
ingot *n.* 铸块；锭

and dollars get *ridged* edges. Workers then check the coins, count them, and put them into bags. Each bag is checked by weighing it. The mints ship the coins to the Federal Reserve Banks. From there, the coins are sent to other banks so they can go into circulation.

们的边缘使其厚一些，最后把图案压印到硬币各面上。十美分、二十五美分、五十美分和一美元硬币的边缘呈脊形状。而后，工人检查硬币，清查数目并装袋。每个袋子都要经过称重检测。铸造局把铸造好的硬币运送到联邦储备银行。这些硬币从那里被送到其他的银行开始进行流通。

ridged　*adj.*　有隆凸线条的；有脊状线的

6

The Susan B. Anthony Dollar

Susan B. Anthony was born in 1820. She grew up in New York, where she began teaching school at 15. At 29, she became a *reformer*. She was against drinking *liquor*, and she worked to help end slavery. She also became a *suffragist*. This means she felt that women should have the same voting rights as men. After the war,

苏珊·布朗奈尔·安东尼—美元硬币

苏珊·布朗奈尔·安东尼出生于1820年。她在纽约长大，十五岁开始在学校任教。29岁时，她成为一名改革家。她反对饮酒，致力于推翻奴隶制度。同时，她是一名妇女政权论者，这表明她主张妇女应和男人拥有相同的选举权。战后，她协助建立了全国妇女选举权协会。该协会的主要目标是修正美国宪法，使妇女拥有选举权。安东尼的余生都

---

reformer *n.* 改革者；改良者　　　　　　liquor *n.* 烈性酒；含酒精饮料
suffragist *n.* 妇女政权论者

she helped found the National Woman Suffrage Association. Its goal was to amend the U.S. Constitution so that women could vote. She worked for the rest of her life to gain the vote.

In 1979 the United States honored Anthony by putting her face on a dollar coin. This was the first time that a woman's portrait was shown on U.S. money. Anthony's face is on the front of the coin. The coin is made from *copper* and nickel over a copper core. The U.S. Mint felt that the coin would replace the dollar bill. It did not turn out that way. The coin is very close in size to a quarter. Many people thought it was easy to confuse the two coins. The mint stopped making the Susan B. Anthony dollar in 1981. But some *vending machines* were built to take the coin, so some people wanted the coins for the machines. The mint made more "Susies" in 1999.

一直在为妇女获得选举权而努力。

为了纪念安东尼，1979年，美国把她的头像印到了一美元硬币上，这是美国的钱币上第一次出现妇女的头像。硬币正面是安东尼的头像。硬币是铜制的，外面用镍包住。美国铸币局本以为该硬币能代替一美元纸币，但事实并非如此。硬币的大小和二十五美分硬币很接近，很多人觉得很容易弄混。1981年，铸币局停止发行苏珊·布朗奈尔·安东尼一美元硬币。但是由于一些自动售卖机的设计接受此硬币，所以人们在使用这种机器时仍需要这种硬币。1999年，铸币局又发行了更多的"安东尼"硬币。

---

copper *n.* 铜   vending machine 投币式自动售货机

7

The Key Responsibilities of Local Government

There are five main levels of local government. One of these is county. States are divided into counties. A county is usually run by a *board* of local people. Two other levels of local government are township (or town) and city. The fourth level of local government is *school district*. School districts do not always have the

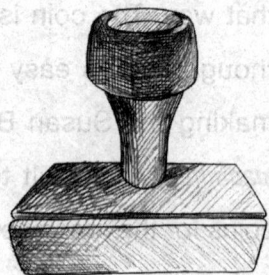

地方政府的主要职责

地方政府主要分为五级。其中之一是县。州可以分成若干个县。县通常由地方委员会治理。地方政府的另外两个级是镇和市，第四级是学区。通常，学区的界限与镇和市不同。一个大城市可能有不止

---

board *n.* 董事会；委员会　　　　　　　　school district 学区

same borders as townships or cities. A large city may have more than one school district. A school district may take in more than one township. The fifth level of local government is special district. This is set up to meet a specific need.

Local governments provide many services. They collect taxes to get money to pay for these services. One service is transportation. Counties and towns build and take care of the local roads. A city must maintain its streets. This includes snow and storm cleanup. Some cities have subways or bus lines that need to be cared for.

Law *enforcement* is a part of local government. A county might have a *sheriff* and *deputies*. A city often has a police force. These law officers enforce the laws and fight crime. There are district, county, and city courts. These courts hear cases. They decide if

---

一个学区，一个学区也可能覆盖不止一个镇。地方政府的第五级是特区，为特殊需要而设立。

地方政府提供许多公共服务。地方政府通过征税来筹集公共服务所需的款项。交通是公共服务中的一项。县和镇共同负责修建并维护本地道路；城市负责维护街道，包括暴风雨、雪后的清理。一些城市还要维护地铁以及公交线路。

法律实施也是地方政府职能的一部分。县有地方治安官和警官，市通常都有自己的警力，他们负责执法并治理犯罪。区、县和市都有地方法

---

enforcement *n.* 执行；实施
deputy *n.* 警官

sheriff *n.* 县治安官；城镇治安官

a person is guilty of breaking a law. They decide how the person should be punished. Communities also have fire departments. Fire departments need fire stations and equipment, such as fire trucks. Large cities may have paid *firefighters* who work full-time. A township might have volunteer firefighters. They are not paid, and they usually work at other jobs.

Local governments provide safe places to play. They pay for and care for parks with playgrounds, sport fields, or pools. Local governments also provide special services for their citizens. They pick up the garbage and provide clean water. They might tell where and how homes may be built. They may have a master plan. This plan shows where businesses and homes may be located. Laws, called *building codes*, state how homes must be built to make sure

院，负责审理案件、判断被告是否犯法并确定刑罚等。社区还有消防队。消防队需要消防站和诸如消防车之类的设备。大城市有全职带薪的消防队员，而镇里可能会有消防志愿者，他们没有报酬，往往从事其他的工作。

地方政府还提供安全的消遣场所。地方政府出钱修建和维护配有游乐场、运动场所以及游泳池的公园。地方政府还为当地居民提供特殊的服务：他们收集垃圾，供应干净的水；他们可以告知居民房屋修建的地点和方法。地方政府有总体的规划，该规划规定商业区和住宅区的坐落情况。

firefighter *n.* 消防队员　　　　building code 建筑法规；建筑条例

they are safe.

School districts *run* the local schools. They hire the teachers and build new schools as needed. A school board receives tax money to pay for the schools. Board members decide how that money should be spent. A special district may run the public libraries. These libraries are free for those who live in the district.

相关法律，即建筑法规，规定了房屋的修建要求，以确保安全。

学区负责管理当地学校。学区负责招聘教师，如有需要，还修建新的学校。税收是校董事会管理学校的资金来源。董事会成员决定资金的使用情况。特区管理当地图书馆，这些图书馆对当地居民免费开放。

run *v.* 管理；经营

8

Becoming a Firefighter

Firefighters are trained professionals who save lives and property. They go into burning buildings. They rescue people who are trapped, scared, or hurt. They teach fire safety in the schools. They save people trapped in car *wrecks* and *cave-ins*. Some are also Emergency Medical Technicians (EMTs). They are trained to help people who are hurt or ill. They help to

如何成为一名消防队员

消防队员是经过专业训练的人士，他们挽救生命和保护财产安全。消防队员进入着火的建筑物，营救受困者、受惊吓者以及伤者。消防队员还去学校教授消防安全知识。他们也营救事故中汽车残骸或倒塌房屋中的受困者。消防队员中一些还是急救医师。他们接受训练，帮助伤者和病人，也协助抢救送往医院途中的人们。

---

wreck *n.* 事故中遭严重毁坏的汽车或飞机等   cave-in *n.* 塌陷；坍塌

keep people alive in route to a hospital.

What kind of person becomes a firefighter? The person must be strong and healthy enough to lift heavy loads, climb ladders, and *crawl* through smoke. He or she must have a sharp mind and calm nerves. This hard job must be done in the face of fires, earthquakes, floods, and accidents.

Who can be a firefighter? Each city or town sets its own standards. But everyone who wants to be a firefighter must finish high school. Then comes special training. EMT classes teach first-aid skills. College classes might include science, math, and building construction. These classes are needed to earn a fire science *certificate*. Then there are written and *oral* tests. If they are passed, there is an *agility* test. This test shows strength and endurance. Once a person is hired, training goes on. Firefighters must learn street names and numbers and the location of schools, factories, and tall buildings.

什么样的人能成为消防队员呢？成为一名消防队员，必须身体健康，体格强壮，足以负载重物，能攀登梯子并在烟雾中爬行。同时，消防员要头脑敏锐并能保持镇定。这份艰难的工作必须在面对大火、地震、洪水和事故的情况下完成。

谁能成为一名消防员呢？每个镇或城市都有自己的标准。但要想成为一名消防队员，首先必须高中毕业。然后就是特殊训练了。急救医师课程教授急救技能。高校课程可能包括理科、数学和房屋建造，这些都是获得消防安全证书的必修课程。还有笔试和口试。这些考试通过后还有敏捷度测验，考察体能和耐力。录取后需要继续训练。消防队员必须熟悉街道名称和门牌号，以及学校、工厂和较高建筑物的地点。

---

crawl *v.* 爬行；匍匐前进
oral *adj.* 口头的

certificate *n.* 证明；合格证书
agility *n.* 敏捷；灵活

9

The Nature of Farming in the United States Today

In the United States today, farms are getting larger in size but fewer in number. In *colonial* America, most people lived on farms. Now less than two percent of the people live on farms.

There are many reasons that fewer people live on farms. One reason is the growth of factories. People moved from

现代美国农业的本质

如今的美国，农场的规模在扩大，但数量在减少。在美国殖民地时期，绝大多数人居住在农场。现在，居住在农场里的人数还不到人口的百分之二。

居住在农场里的人数减少的原因有很多。一是由于工厂的发展。就业

colonial *adj.* 殖民的；英属殖民地时期的

farms to cities because jobs were available. Another reason is the use of machines on the farm. One of the first farm machines was the McCormick *reaper*. It reduced the labor needed to harvest wheat. More farm machines followed. They could do bigger jobs with fewer workers. Another change is that more food can be grown per acre. This is because of new *strains* of crops and better farming methods.

Farming has moved into world trade. Farmers grow more food than is needed in the United States. They sell some of what they produce overseas. But they must sell at prices that can compete in the world market. Large farms can produce more at a lower cost. They can get better buys on *inputs*, such as seed and *fertilizer*. Large farms use the latest farm machines to work more acres. Where do large farms get more land? They buy up farms that go out of

机会的增多使得人们从农场迁往城市；另一个原因则是农业机器的应用。麦考密克收割机是最早使用的农业机械之一，它减少了小麦收割所需的劳动力。还有很多其他的农业机械，它们能用较少的劳动力完成更大型的任务。另一个变化是由于作物新品种以及更好的种植方法的引进而带来的粮食亩产量增加。

农业已经进入了世界贸易领域。在美国，农民生产的粮食供大于求，于是一些粮食销往海外，但是所出售粮食的价格必须在世界市场上具有竞争力才行。大型农场能以较低的投入获得更多的产出：诸如种子、化肥等农业投入，他们往往购买得更划算、更实惠。而且，大型农场使用最新的

reaper *n.* 收割机
input *n.* 投入；输入

strain *n.* （动、植物的）系；品种
fertilizer *n.* 肥料

business, or they rent land. A farm of 4,000 acres might actually be several small farms spread over several counties.

Small and medium-size farms cannot compete with large farms in the world market. In the past 20 years, many medium-size farms have disappeared. The farms have either grown in size or been sold. But the number of small farms has stayed about the same. How do small farms survive? The farmers have other means of income. They may work other jobs so they can run their farms on the side. They choose to farm even though profits are not high. Small farms have found their own markets. They may specialize in *organic* milk or fancy jams. Some sell directly to the public. They might have a roadside *stand*, a petting farm, a gift shop, or a *cider mill*. Sometimes small farms band together to work like a large farm. They may form

农业机械，这样能耕种更多的土地。那么这些大型农场从哪儿得到更多的土地呢？他们通过收购破产的农场或是租地获得更多的土地。一个占地4000英亩的农场实际上可能是由分布在几个县的若干小农场组成。

小农场和中型农场无法与大型农场在国际市场中抗衡。在过去的20年里，很多中型农场都消失了，有的发展壮大，有的则被收购了。然而，小农场的数目还和20年前差不多。那么，小农场是如何幸存下来的呢？原来，这些农民有其他的收入来源。他们从事其他的工作，经营农场只是他们的副业。尽管利润不高，他们还是选择经营农场。小农场有自己的市场：他们可能擅长生产有机奶和可口的果酱，其中一些直接面向公众销

organic *adj.* 有机的；绿色的　　　　　　stand *n.* 货摊；售货亭
cider *n.* 苹果酒；苹果汁　　　　　　　　mill *n.* 制造厂；工厂

a cooperative to buy farm machines. They may buy inputs in large amounts. Some small farms may form a larger *corporation*. Small, medium, or large, about 99 percent of U.S. farms are still owned by families.

售；他们也可能有个路边摊位、宠物农场、礼品店或苹果酒工厂。有时小农场也联合起来像大型农场那样运作。他们可能成立一个合作社，一起购买农业机械，也可能大量地购买农业投入物。一些小农场还可能成立一个更大的公司。但无论小农场、中型农场还是大型农场，约99%的美国农场都归家庭所有。

corporation *n.* 企业；大公司

10

The McCormick Reaper

In the early 1800s, it took a lot of *manual* labor to harvest wheat. First, the wheat was cut with a cradle. This was a long wooden handle with a cutting *blade* and wooden fingers. The farmer swung the cradle side to side. The blade cut the wheat, and the fingers held it. The farmer dropped the *stalks* of wheat in piles. Next,

麦考密克收割机

十九世纪初，小麦收割需要大量的手工劳作。首先，用配禾架镰刀把小麦割下来。这种镰刀有个长长的木头柄，上面带有刀片和木抓手。农民左右挥舞大镰刀，刀片割下麦子，木抓手把麦子接住。农民把割下的麦秆堆成堆，然后，捆成捆。最后，一捆捆的麦子立着放到一起，称作麦垛。一人一天能割大约两英亩的麦子。麦粒干透后，进行打谷

---

manual *adj.* 手工的；体力的   blade *n.* 刀身；刀片
stalk *n.* 茎；秆

the stalks were tied in *bundles*. Finally, the bundles were stood up in groups, called *shocks*. One worker could cradle about two acres per day. After the grain dried, it was *threshed*, or removed from the stalks.

About 1831 Cyrus McCormick of Virginia invented a mechanical reaper. It was pulled by a horse. Blades moved back and forth to cut the grain. A wide wheel supported the machine as it rolled along. The wheel turned a reel that pushed the cut grain onto a platform. One worker rode the horse. Another raked the grain from the platform. The reaper could cut as much grain in one day as five workers could cut with cradles. McCormick moved to Chicago and started a company. He improved his machine. His Harvester and Binder cut grain and bound it with *twine*. Today's farm machines can cut 50 acres per day. They can also thresh the grain and clean it.

或者脱粒。

　　大约在1831年时，弗吉尼亚州的赛勒斯·麦考密克发明了一种机械收割机。这个收割机由一匹马拉着，刀片前后移动把谷物割下。机器转动行进的过程中有一个宽轮子支撑着它，这个轮子转动一个卷轴把割下的谷物推到平台上。一名工人骑着马，另一名工人耙平台上的谷物。一台收割机一天收割的谷物相当于五个农民用大镰刀收割的工作量。后来，麦考密克搬到了芝加哥并创办了一个公司。他改进了机器，割捆机能把谷物割下来并用线扎成捆。现在的农业机械每天的工作面积达到了50英亩，能脱粒并能清洁谷物。

---

bundle *n.* （一）捆；包　　　　　　shock *n.* 禾束堆；一堆
thresh *v.* 使脱粒　　　　　　　　　twine *n.* 绳；线

11

The One-Room Schoolhouse of the Nineteenth Century

In the United States in the nineteenth century, many children were taught in one-room *schoolhouses*. Grades one through eight shared the same classroom. A typical one-room schoolhouse was built of wood and painted white or red.

To get to school, children walked, rode a horse, or rode in a *buggy*. When it was time for school to begin, the teacher rang a bell.

"只有一间教室" ——十九世纪的美国校舍

在十九世纪，许多美国孩子都在只有一间教室的校舍里学习过。一年级到八年级共用一间教室。一个典型的"只有一间教室"的校舍是一幢刷成白色或红色的木头房子。

孩子们或步行，或骑马，或坐轻便马车上学。到上课时间，教师打

---

schoolhouse *n.* （尤指旧时乡村学校的）校舍   buggy *n.* 轻便马车

The children then went inside. Sometimes they stopped in a small room to wash their hands. They poured water from a pitcher into a bowl, called a basin. They hung their coats on hooks in a *cloakroom* and then went to their desks. They stood to recite the Pledge of Allegiance. The smallest children sat in the smallest desks at the front of the room, nearest the teacher's desk. The tallest children sat in the back. In the middle of the room stood a *potbellied* stove. It was used for heat on cold days. Those near the stove may have felt too warm. Those farthest away may have felt cold. The stove burned fuel, such as wood or coal.

The subjects taught were *arithmetic*, geography, science, history, reading, art, and *penmanship*. Students learned to write beautiful flowing script that was easy to read. Teachers wrote lessons on a blackboard at the front of the room. That is also where students worked math problems or practiced writing. In some schools,

---

铃。随后孩子们进入教室。有时候孩子们会在一个房间停下来，把水壶里的水倒到盆里洗手，衣服挂到衣帽间，然后走到自己的桌子前，站立着背诵宣誓效忠词。最小的孩子坐到教室前面最小的桌子前，离老师最近。最高的孩子坐在教室后面。教室的中间有一个炉膛很大的火炉，天气寒冷时，用于取暖。坐在炉子附近的孩子可能会觉得太热，而坐得远的又可能觉得冷。炉子烧的是诸如木头和煤这类的燃料。

　　教授的课程包括算术、地理、科学、历史、阅读、艺术以及书法。学生们学习写易于阅读的手写体文字，要求漂亮、流畅。教师用教室前面的黑板讲课。孩子们也用那块黑板解数学题或练习书法。有些学校的孩子有

---

cloakroom *n.* 衣帽间；衣帽寄放处
arithmetic *n.* 算术；算术运算

potbellied *adj.* 肚子大的；啤酒肚的
penmanship *n.* 书法；书写艺术

students had their own small *slates* to write on. Because one teacher had to teach all grade levels, the children were often taught one at a time.

Children were expected to be well behaved. Those who were not were punished by the teacher. The teacher may have used a leather strap, wooden *cane*, or wooden *paddle* for this purpose. Sometimes a child who had misbehaved would have to cut a switch from a tree, which the teacher would use on him or her. At noon, there was a *recess*. The children played and ate lunch. Students often carried their lunch to school in metal pails. In very cold weather, the teacher might cook something hot on the stove. Lessons resumed in the afternoon. When school let out, the children went home. There was rarely homework. Children were expected to help at home or do farm chores. Only a few children owned books. Books carried to and from school were wrapped by a leather strap and carried by the loose end of the strap.

自己的练习小石板。由于一名老师要教授所有年级的课程，所以一次课只能针对一个年级。

孩子们应该举止得体，举止不当的孩子会受到老师的惩罚。老师可能用皮鞭、木杖或木头戒尺惩罚学生。有时，犯错误的学生得自己从树上砍下个枝条作为鞭子，老师会用它惩罚学生。午休时间，孩子们吃午饭、玩耍。通常，孩子们用金属制的提桶把午餐带到学校。天气非常冷时，老师会用炉子煮点热东西。下午继续上课。放学后孩子们就回家了。很少有课后作业，孩子们要帮家里做家务或做点农活。只有少部分学生有书。书用皮带捆扎好，学生们拎着皮带松着的一端往返于学校和家里。

---

slate *n.* （旧时学生用于写字的）石板   cane *n.* 竹杖；藤条

paddle *n.* 戒尺   recess *n.* 课间休息；间歇

12

The McGuffey Readers

*T*he McGuffey Readers were textbooks that were used in schools in the United States in the nineteenth century. These were books of stories, poems, speeches, and *essays*. The readings were happy in *tone* so they would appeal to children. William McGuffey developed the books. He was a teacher from Ohio. The books were used to teach reading, writing, and spelling. They also

《麦加菲读本》

《麦加菲读本》是十九世纪美国学校所使用的教科书，包括故事、诗歌、演讲和短文等。该读本语气欢快，孩子们很感兴趣。它是由俄亥俄州的一名教师——威廉·麦加菲——编写，可以用来教授阅读、写作、拼写以及道德规范等。读本强调诚实、仁爱和勤奋。这些价值

---

essay *n.* 短文；论说文   tone *n.* 语气；口吻

taught moral values. The readings stressed honesty, charity, and hard work. These values often stayed with students long after they had grown up.

There were seven books in all. Each one was on a different reading level. Students began with the first book. It was called *The Eclectic First Reader for Young Children*. The word eclectic refers to the mix of stories and poems. When a student finished one book, he or she began the next. Students read the books at their own speed. A twelve-year-old and an eight-year-old might be on the same book. A student could graduate from school when he or she had read all the books.

The books had *charts* that showed how to say basic sounds. There was a list of new words at the start of each lesson. The books were *illustrated* with pictures.

The McGuffey Readers were first published in 1836. Although not used in today's schools, they are still available.

观即使在孩子们成年后也会一直伴随着他们。

《麦加菲读本》共七册，每一册代表不同的阅读级别。学生们从第一册学起。第一册叫做《幼儿启蒙读本》。"Eclectic"指这本书里既有故事又有诗歌。学生学完一册后就开始学下一册。学生们以自己的速度阅读，一个十二岁的孩子可能和一个八岁的孩子读同一册书。学完所有的教材后学生们就毕业了。

读本中配有图表教孩子们如何发音。每一课的开头都有生词表。读本中还配有插图。

《麦加菲读本》于1836年首次出版。尽管现在学校不再使用了，但人们还能找到这套书。

electic *adj.* 不拘一格的；兼收并蓄的　　　　　　　　chart *n.* 图表
illustrate *v.* 加插图于；给（书等）做图表

13

The Kimono: Traditional Dress of Japan

The word kimono refers to traditional Japanese dress. The word comes from kiru (which means "to wear") and mono (which means "thing"). Men, women, and children all wear kimonos.

The basic kimono is a *robe* that hangs from the shoulders to the *heels*. It has square-cut *sleeves* and an open front that

和服:日本传统服装

和服一词指的是日本的传统民族服装。它由日语"kiru"（穿）和"mono"（物品）这两个词组合派生而成。男人、女人和孩子都穿和服。

和服主要是一件从肩膀一直垂到脚跟的长袍。衣袖是正方形剪裁,

---

robe *n.* 袍服;礼袍
sleeve *n.* 袖子

heel *n.* 足跟;脚后跟

overlaps. All adult robes are made from one long, narrow length of fabric. The *fabric* width is not cut. It is sewn with wide or narrow seams to fit the wearer's shape. More than one robe may be worn at the same time.

The color, pattern, fabric, sleeve length, and sleeve shape depend on the wearer, the season, and the occasion. Women's sleeves are rounded. Men's sleeves are straight. Young girls wear bright colors and quite long sleeves. Unmarried women wear kimonos with large brightly colored designs and long sleeves. A bride may wear a white under-kimono and an over-kimono with a colored design. Some brides wear a set of four robes. Married women wear darker colors and shorter sleeves. Older women wear very dark colors and shorter sleeves. Men wear dark robes with a *faint* pattern or thin *stripes*. The

---

前襟可以左右开合。所有成人和服的袍体部分都是由一块长方形的面料做成，面料的宽幅并不做剪裁。和服的肥瘦取决于缝口边线的宽窄，以适合穿戴者的体型。一个人可以同时穿几件和服。

不同的穿着者、不同的季节、不同的场合决定了和服的颜色、款式、用料以及袖子的长度和形状。女式和服的袖子是圆形的。男式和服袖子是直的。女孩子穿的振袖和服颜色亮丽，长袖飘飘。未婚女子所穿的振袖和服色彩明亮、款式大方，也是长袖飘飘。新娘里面穿白色和服，外面穿的和服则是彩色的。有些新娘还会穿一种四件套的礼服。已婚女子穿的留袖和服则袖子短些，颜色暗些。上了年纪的女性所穿的和服往往袖子更短，颜色更暗。男式

---

fabric *n.* 织物；布料
stripe *n.* 条纹；线条

faint *adj.* 不积极的；淡淡的

most formal robes are made of silk and have five family *crests*, called mon. Less formal robes may have three mon. The most informal robes are cotton. They are worn in summer.

A kimono is closed with a *sash*, called an obi. Men's obi are narrow and plain. They wrap around the body and tie in the back. Women's obi come in many lengths, widths, colors, and designs. They tie in the back with a special *bow*. Extra pieces are needed to tie the sash. These give it volume, make it lay flat, and help it keep its shape.

A formal kimono for a woman may have 10 pieces. She may need help to dress. A formal *outfit* for a man includes a hakama (skirt-trouser) and a haori (short jacket). These are worn over the kimono. Women may also wear these pieces, but they never wear both at the same time.

和服经常带有淡淡图案或细细条纹, 颜色为深色。最正式的和服礼服由丝绸制成, 绣有日语称为 "mon" 的五个家纹; 一般正式的和服礼服上只绣三个家纹; 最不正式的便装和服则是棉质的, 一般在夏天穿着。

　　和服用腰带束起, 这种腰带日语叫做 "obi"。男子的腰带是素色窄带, 腰带从前面绕过身体系在身后。不同长度、不同宽幅、不同颜色以及不同图案的女子腰带在背后系成一个特别的蝴蝶结, 还需要一些额外的和服配件系在腰带之外, 以保证和服的整体效果, 平整并且有形。

　　一件正式的女式和服有10个和服配饰。女士在穿着时需要有人帮忙。正式的男式礼服套装包括 "hakama" （裙裤）和 "haori" （短上

---

crest *n.* 饰章; 纹章　　　　　　　　　sash *n.* 腰带; 饰带
bow *n.* 蝴蝶结　　　　　　　　　　　　outfit *n.* 全套服装; 装束

Formal kimonos are worn with *zori*. These *sandals* have a *thong* that divides the big toe from the rest of the toes. They are worn with split-toe socks called tabi.

Today kimonos are usually worn only at special times. While at work or play, most Japanese wear western-style clothes.

衣），都穿在和服外面。女子也会穿裙裤和短上衣，不过绝对不会同时穿两样。

正式的和服礼服要搭配日式草履来穿。这种鞋上有一个带，把大脚趾和其他的脚趾分开。这种鞋与日语中称为 "tabi" 的分趾袜搭配穿着。

如今，日本人通常只在特殊的场合才穿和服。工作和娱乐中，绝大多数日本人穿西式服装。

---

zori *n.* 草履；便鞋   sandal *n.* 凉鞋；便鞋

thong *n.* 皮带

14

Shichi-go-san: The Festival Day for Children in Japan

Shichi-go-san is Japanese for "seven, five, three". Shichi-go-san is a special day for boys ages three and five and girls ages three and seven. On November 15, parents take children of these ages to a *shrine*. There a *priest* says *prayers* for their healthy growth. Children wear *ceremonial* dress on this day. Before

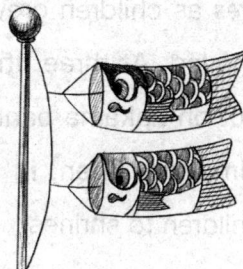

7-5-3：日本儿童节

"Shichi-go-san" 是日语的 "7，5，3"，是日本3岁和5岁的男孩、3岁和7岁的女孩的一个特殊日子。11月15日这一天，这几个年龄的孩子的父母会带着他们去神社。在那里，僧人会为孩子们的健康成长祈福。这一天，孩子们要穿庆典礼服。女孩们去神社前要穿上和

---

shrine *n.* 圣地；神庙　　　　priest *n.* 教士；僧侣
prayer *n.* 祈祷文；经文　　　ceremonial *adj.* 用于礼仪的；礼节的

they go to the shrine, girls dress in kimonos. Boys dress in haori jackets and hakama pants. After prayers at the shrine, parents buy their children longevity candy. This shows that they wish for their children to live a long, long time. The candy is called chitose-ame, which means "1,000 years". It is made in long sticks that are red and white. It comes in a long bag with pictures of *cranes* and *turtles*. These animals are also the sign of long life.

The day has its roots in *medieval* times. Important families held *rites* as children grew. Up to age three, children's heads were kept shaved. At three, the hair was left to grow. At age five, boys first put on hakama pants. At age seven, girls first used obi to tie their kimonos. Then, in later years, all classes of families took their children to shrines.

服，男孩们则要穿上羽织上衣和裙袴。在神社接受祈福后，父母们会给孩子买长寿糖，这代表他们希望他们的孩子可以长寿。这种糖叫做"千岁糖"，顾名思义，指"一千岁"。糖是红白色的棒棒，装在一个印有鹤和乌龟图案的长袋子里，这些动物也是长寿的象征。

这个特殊日子的起源可追溯到中世纪。那时达官贵人家会为孩子举行成长仪式。孩子在三岁前，头发一直剃光。到了三岁，开始留发。五岁时，男孩首次穿上裙袴。七岁时，女孩首次用腰带束起和服。后来，各阶层的家庭都会带他们的孩子去神社。

---

crane *n.* 鹤   turtle *n.* 龟
medieval *adj.* 中世纪的   rite *n.* 仪式；典礼

15

What Is a Region in the United States?

A region is an area that has similar *features*. These features make the region different from other areas. A region may have similar culture, history, or climate. It may have similar *landforms*, such as hills, valleys, or plains. It may have a similar function—that is, it may have many large cities or a lot of farmland. There are no set boundaries for regions. Sometimes the

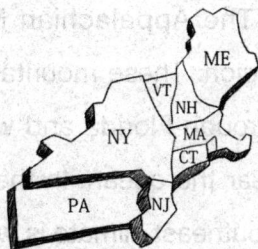

什么是美国的行政区？

行政区是一片有相似特征的区域。这些特征使得一个行政区和其他地区有所不同。一个行政区会有相似的文化、历史或者气候。区内会有诸如丘陵、山谷或平原一类的相似地貌。它在功能上也很相似——换言之，区内可能会有很多大城市或者有很多的大农场。区和区之间没有设定边界。有时，美国分为五大区，分别是东北区、东南区、中西

---

feature *n.* 特征；特色　　　　　　　　　　landform *n.* 地形；地貌

United States is divided up into five very large regions. These regions are the Northeast, Southeast, Midwest, Southwest, and West.

The Northeast region includes the area from Maine to Maryland and from the Atlantic Ocean to Pennsylvania. Near the ocean is a flat strip of land called a *coastal* plain. Most of the big cities are found there. Fishing is important to this area. The region is known for its seafood. Inland are the Appalachian Mountains. The climate of the Northeast has four seasons.

The Appalachian Mountains continue through the Southeast region. These mountains are rich in coal. This region spreads south through Florida and west through Arkansas. The coastal plains are near the ocean. In the south are the *swamps* of the Everglades. The Southeast climate is warm. There is a long season for growing crops.

The Midwest is flat and good for farming. Some Midwest states are near the Great Lakes. They have big cities and big industries.

部区、西南部区和西部区。

　　东北区是辖缅因州到马里兰州，大西洋到宾夕法尼亚州的一片区域。靠近大西洋的一片平整的狭长地带称为海岸平原，多数的大城市都聚集在此区。捕鱼业是这一地区的重中之重，这里的海鲜闻名遐迩。内陆是阿巴拉契亚山脉。整个东北区四季分明。

　　阿巴拉契亚山脉绵延穿过整个东南区。这些山脉煤矿资源丰富。东南区向南纵贯佛罗里达州，向西横穿阿肯色州。近海地区是大面积的平原，国家公园的大片沼泽地就在南部。东南部气候温暖，适合作物生长的季节很长。

　　中西部区地貌平整，适合农场经营。此区的一些州位于五大湖附近，有很多大都市和大型产业。其他州位于平原地区。其中，中部平原雨水充

---

coastal *adj.* 沿海的；靠近海岸的　　　　　　　　**swamp** *n.* 沼泽地

The other states are on the plains. The Central Plains get plenty of rain. Much corn is grown there. The Great Plains are drier. Wheat grows there. The Midwest has a climate with four seasons.

The Southwest shares a border with Mexico. The climate is dry. There are deserts, mountains, and *canyons*. It is warm in the deserts and cold in the mountains. The Four Corners region is where four states meet. They are Arizona, New Mexico, Utah, and Colorado.

Alaska and Hawaii are two states in the West. The rest of the states in the West are in two groups. The Mountain States have the Rocky Mountains. Winters there are long and cold. The Pacific States lie next to the Pacific Ocean. The Central Valley of California has rich farmland. It is warm there, and crops are grown year round. In the northwest part of this region, it can be warm but wet. There are rain forests with very tall trees. *Lumber* and wood products come from the West.

沛，适合多数作物生长；大平原地区则相对干旱，出产小麦。中西部区四季分明。

西南区和墨西哥接壤，气候干燥，有沙漠、山，也有峡谷。沙漠地区气候温暖，山区寒冷。四角地区就是四个州——亚利桑那州、新墨西哥州、犹他州和科罗拉多州——的交汇之处。

阿拉斯加州和夏威夷州是位于西部区的两个州。西部区的其他州主要分为两大类：一些地处山区的州主要位于落基山脉，那里冬季漫长而寒冷；地处太平洋沿岸的各州毗邻太平洋。佛罗里达州的中部峡谷有肥沃的耕地，那里气候温暖，作物全年生长。西部区的西北部气候温暖湿润，形成有高大树木生长的雨林。西部区是木材和木制品的生产地。

---

canyon *n.* 峡谷

lumber *n.* 林木；木材

16

The Rocky Mountain Region of the United States

Parts of Montana, Idaho, Wyoming, Utah, and Colorado have high, *rugged* mountain *ranges*. These ranges are all part of the Rocky Mountains. The Rockies were formed millions of years ago as pressure *heaved* up Earth's *crust*. Water running down the peaks carved out deep canyons. Later, glaciers shaped sharp

美国的落基山脉区

蒙大拿州、爱达荷州、怀俄明州、犹他州和科罗拉多州的部分地区地势高，位于崎岖不平的山区，都属落基山脉的山系。数百万年前，巨大的压力挤压地壳隆起形成了落基山脉。从峰顶而下的水刻出了深深的峡谷。后来，冰川形成了陡峭的山峰和宽阔的山谷。如今，一些山峰上仍有长年不化的冰帽。这些山脉盛产矿石：煤矿、铜矿、金矿、

---

rugged *adj.* 崎岖的
heave *n.* 举起；拉

range *n.* 山脉
crust *n.* 硬层；硬表面

peaks and broad valleys. Today there are still permanent ice caps on some peaks. The mountains are rich in minerals. Coal, copper, gold, iron *ore*, lead, and silver are mined here. The valleys are home to cattle and sheep *ranches*. The mountains are home to many kinds of wildlife. *Elk*, bears, moose, deer, beavers, and mountain goats live here. Lumber is cut from mountain forests.

The region has long cold winters and short summers. As one climbs a mountain, the temperature becomes colder. In this region, there are few cities. The small population is *sparse*, or spread out. Tourists come to the region in winter to ski. They come in summer to climb, hike, fish, camp, and raft on rushing rivers. The region has several parks. One of these is Yellowstone National Park. Here visitors can see geysers and hot springs. These are the result of a live volcano. Almost half of the park lies in a crater formed from an eruption.

铁矿、铅矿和银矿都有。山谷则是牛群羊群的大牧场。落基山也是很多野生动物的家园，麋鹿、熊、驼鹿、梅花鹿、海狸和北美野山羊都生活在这里。落基山脉也是主要的木材供应地。

　　这一地区冬季漫长而夏季短暂。越往山顶温度越低。这里几乎没什么城市，人口稀少，居住分散。这里是冬季滑雪的好去处，夏季人们来这里爬山、徒步、垂钓、露营，并在湍急的河水中漂流。这里还有公园，其中之一就是黄石国家公园。游客们可以在黄石公园看到由活火山喷发后形成的间歇喷泉和温泉。整个公园几乎一半的地方都坐落在火山喷发形成的火山口上。

---

ore *n.* 矿；矿石　　　　　　　　ranch *n.* 牧场；大农场
elk *n.* 驼鹿；麋鹿　　　　　　　sparse *adj.* 稀少的；稀疏的

17

How Does Folklore Help Us Learn about the Past?

Every culture has its own *folklore*. These tales and bits of wisdom teach children how to behave and what to believe. Folklore includes legends, songs, art, tales, myths, and *proverbs*. It is handed down from one generation to the next.

Folklore helps keep history alive. Legends are folktales that are based on

民间传说怎样帮助我们了解过去呢？

每一种文化都有自己的民间传说。这些故事和条条智慧之语教导孩子们如何处世和信仰什么。民间传说代代相传，它包括传奇故事、歌曲、艺术、传说、神话和谚语。

民间传说使历史保持鲜活。传奇故事是在真实故事基础上衍生出来的民间传说。只不过真实平白的历史往往不那么有趣，讲故事的人为了听者的兴趣就会编撰细节。故事更加生动有趣，人们也越发乐于口口相传。这

---

folklore *n.* 民间传统；民间传说   proverb *n.* 谚语；格言

true stories. But the plain truth about history is not always exciting. So the storyteller invents details to keep the listener's interest. The tale becomes so interesting that it gets retold. Thus, a legend is born. One such legend is about Davy Crockett. Davy Crockett lived in the *backwoods* of the frontier. He became a *statesman*, and he fought in a war with Mexico. His brave deeds were *exaggerated* in stories. He came to stand for the spirit of the frontier. Children loved the tales. They learned about frontier life through stories about Davy Crockett.

Tall tales are folktales that stretch the truth. They are sometimes told to fool those who hear them. There are many tall tales of the American West. An example of a tall tale is the story about Paul Bunyan, the giant *lumberjack*. It is said that his clothes were so large

---

样，传奇故事就诞生了。关于大卫·克洛科特的传说就是一个典型事例。大卫·克洛科特生活在边远落后的地区，他后来成为了政治家，还参加了对墨西哥的战争。传奇故事中夸大了大卫的英勇行为，他成为了美国边疆的精神象征。孩子们都喜欢关于他的传奇故事，他们通过大卫·克洛科特的故事了解到边疆的生活。

荒诞不经的故事是夸大事实的民间传说。这样的故事有时候是为了愚弄听故事的人。关于美国西部就有许多这样的故事。一个这类奇谈的例子就是保罗·班杨，美国伐木巨人的故事。据说他的衣服大到每个衬衫纽扣都是四轮马车的车轮子。关于他的传说背景都是他伐木的营地。这类故事

---

backwoods *n.* 边远落后地区
exaggerated *adj.* 夸张的；夸大的

statesman *n.* 政治家
lumberjack *n.* 伐木工；木材采运工

that his shirt buttons were *wagon* wheels. Tales about Bunyan are set at his lumber camp. The tales are fun to hear. They also show what life was like in a lumber camp.

Myths are folktales that tell how the universe was made. They tell where the first humans came from. Myths are about gods or *divine* beings in human or animal form. People who told myths thought the stories were true—and so did the listeners. Myths can teach us about people's beliefs and values.

Fairy tales may also tell us more about a culture. These folktales are not believed by the teller or by the audience. They are tales such as "*Snow White*" or "*The Three Little Pigs*". They often begin with the words "Once upon a time …" The same tale may exist in different forms in more than one culture.

听起来很过瘾，也向人们展现了伐木营地的生活。

神话是关于宇宙如何形成的这类民间传说。它们会告诉我们最早的人类来自哪里。神话也是关于那些人或者动物形象的造物主和诸神的故事。讲神话的人相信这些故事是真的，听者也同样相信这一点。神话故事能让我们了解到人们的信仰和价值观。

童话故事也可以告诉我们更多关于文化方面的东西。讲童话的人和听童话的人都不会真的相信这类故事，比如《白雪公主》或《三只小猪》。童话故事一般都以 "很久以前……" 开头。同样的故事可能会在不一样的文化里以不一样的形式出现。

---

wagon *n.* 四轮载重马车（或牛车）   divine *adj.* 上帝的；神的
fairy tale 童话故事

Studying folklore is one way to learn about a culture. People who study folklore are called *folklorists*. Folklorists look at more than just folktales. They look at folk art, folk music, poetry, and proverbs. A proverb is a wise saying such as "The early bird gets the worm." Proverbs are used to teach children the wisdom of their elders.

研究民间传说是一种了解文化的方式。研究民间传说的人被称为民俗研究者，他们不单单研究民间传说，还研究民间艺术、民间音乐、民间诗歌和民间谚语。谚语是人类智慧的结晶，比如"早起的鸟儿有虫吃。"通过谚语，孩子们可以学到先辈们的智慧。

folklorist n. 民俗学研究者；民俗学家

18

Johnny Appleseed: The Man and the Legend

John Chapman was born in Massachusetts about 1774. He grew up to be a *gardener*. He planted apple trees in New York and Pennsylvania. In the early 1800s, he carried apple seeds west. He walked the *wilderness* that would later become Michigan, Ohio, Indiana, and Illinois. When he found a good place for

苹果种子约翰尼：一个人的传说

约翰·查普曼大约在1774年出生于美国马萨诸塞州。长大成人后他做了一名花匠，并在纽约和宾夕法尼亚州种植苹果树。19世纪早期，他把苹果种子带到西部。他走过一片荒蛮之地——后来成为密歇根州、俄亥俄州、印第安纳州和伊利诺斯州。沿途每当他发现适合种植苹果树的地方，就把灌木丛清理干净，一排一排地播撒苹果种子，还为这些苹果种子架起藩篱。起初，他返回东部取来更多的种子，后来他就可以从自己亲手栽下的苹果树上取种子了。他一路步行穿过荒野，一路照料着他

---

gardener n. 园丁；花匠；菜农　　　　wilderness n. 荒芜的地方；未开发的地区

apple trees, he cleared the brush. He planted the seeds in rows. Then he *fenced* them in. At first he went back east for more seeds. Later he got seeds from the trees he grew. He *roamed* through the wilderness, tending to his *orchards*. He traveled on foot, often without shoes. He carried with him a cooking pot.

When the first settlers came, Chapman sold his trees for pennies. Sometimes he traded them for used clothes. The settlers called him Johnny Appleseed. Those who moved on west told of the man who sold them the trees. The tale passed down through the generations. More tales were added to the legend. In one tale, Johnny Appleseed slept through a storm with a bear. In another, a *rattlesnake* tried to bite his foot, but his skin was too tough. In books, he might be shown in clothes that are too big, wearing his pot as a hat. Some of the trees he planted still bear fruit today.

的片片果园。而且，他经常赤足而走，随身带着一口锅。

当第一批拓荒者到达时，查普曼把他的果树卖给他们换一些钱。有时候，他也卖果树换一些旧衣服。拓荒者称他为：苹果种子约翰尼。西行的拓荒者们口传着他的故事——卖给他们果树的人的故事。这个传奇故事代代相传，并且传说中又被新添了许多故事。其中一个说：约翰尼曾经和大熊一起共眠渡过一场暴风雨。另一个故事里，响尾蛇试图咬他的脚，但他脚上的皮太硬了，没能成功。在书中，人们可能会描绘约翰尼穿着过大的衣服，头上顶着一个锅当做帽子。到今天，他种下的很多苹果树仍然结着苹果。

---

fence *v.* 用（栅栏、篱笆或围栏）围住
orchard *n.* 果园

roam *v.* 闲逛；漫步
rattlesnake *n.* 响尾蛇

19

El Pueblo: The Birthplace of the City of Angels

In the late eighteenth century, Spain ruled Mexico. California also belonged to Spain. It was a vast place with scattered native *tribes* and a few Spanish *missions*. Britain and Russia tried to move in on the land. Felipe de Neve was California's *governor*. He thought a new town might help solve the problem. It would improve Spain's

普埃布洛: 天使之城的诞生地

18世纪末，西班牙统治着墨西哥。加利福尼亚也隶属西班牙，那一大片土地上有一些分散的本地部落以及几个西班牙传教团。英国和俄国试图介入这片土地，未果。费利佩·德·内夫是当时加利福尼亚的总督。他认为建个新城也许能解决这个问题，这样能加强西班牙对这

---

tribe *n.* 部落

governor *n.* 总督；管辖者

mission *n.* 传教；布道团

claim to the land. Food could be grown there for Spain's troops. Up to that time, food had to be brought in by ship. De Neve chose a site on a low plain. It was by the ocean and on the Los Angeles River.

Finding settlers for the new town was a problem. People did not want to go there, even for free land and *livestock*. The search for settlers took months. At last, de Neve found 12 families. They were Native Americans, Africans, Spaniards, and people of mixed race. In 1781 they reached the site. They named it El Pueblo de la Reina de Los Angeles. The name means "the Town of the Queen of the Angels".

In the first years, they built a *plaza*, or town square. Buildings were made of sun-dried brick, called *adobe*. Land *grants* were given to soldiers. Cattle was raised on the first ranches. The first orange

---

片土地的所有权，而且还可以在这片土地上种植作物，为军队提供食物补给。那时候，食物还需用船引进。德·内夫在低平原上选了一块地方，它靠近海洋，而且这里还有洛杉矶河。

为新城找到定居者是个难题。即使馈赠土地和家畜，人们也并不想去这个地方。为了找到定居者，几个月过去了。最后，德·内夫寻到了12户人家愿意来此定居。这些人有美洲土著人、非洲人、西班牙人和其他的混血人种。1781年，这些人到达了此地。他们称此地为"El Pueblo de la Reina de Los Angeles"，意思是"天使女王之城"。

在最初的几年里，他们建了一个广场，即城市广场。城中的建筑物都

---

livestock *n.* 牲畜；家畜　　　　plaza *n.* 露天广场
adobe *n.* （建筑用）黏土；黏土坯　　grant *n.* （政府、机构的）授予物

grove in California was planted. At about this time, California was *split*—Baja was in the south, and Alta was in the north. El Pueblo was part of Alta.

In 1821 Mexico broke free of Spain. The new governors gave more land grants in Alta to new *settlers*. Some of these settlers came by ship from the East Coast or from Europe. More came by *wagon train*. They started businesses and ranches. In 1846 the United States went to war with Mexico. After the war, Alta became the state of California. When gold was found in California, El Pueblo sold food to the miners.

For the next 30 years, the people of Los Angeles kept their Mexican traditions. Spanish was still the main language. This changed as people from other cultures came. The railroad opened new markets for trade. It also brought more people. Numbers of

---

是由太阳晒干的泥砖即黏土坯建成。土地分给了士兵。最早的大牧场用来养牛。加利福尼亚也种植了第一个橘子园。与此同时,加利福尼亚一分为二,南部称为 "Baja"(低),北部称为 "Alta"(高)。普埃布洛是 "Alta" 的一部分。

1821年,墨西哥从西班牙解放出来。新总督给予新来的定居者更多在 "Alta" 的土地所有权。这群人中有些从东海岸乘船到达这里,有些从欧洲乘船而来,更多的人则是乘坐马车。他们开始贸易往来或者是建设农场。1846年,美国和墨西哥交战。战后,"Alta" 变成了加利福尼亚州。在加利福尼亚发现金矿后,普埃布洛主要向开矿者出售食物。

随后的30年里,洛杉矶城的人们都保持他们的墨西哥传统,而且西

---

split *v.* 分开   settler *n.* 移民;殖民者
wagon train 车队;马车队

Chinese, French, and Italian settlers came. Later the movie business came to the city. During World War II, the city's factories made things needed for the war. Workers came for jobs. Farms were turned into *suburbs*. Today Los Angeles is the second-largest city in the United States.

班牙语仍然是主要的语言，直到有来自其他文化的人们的到来。铁路为贸易的发展开辟了新的市场，也带来了更多的人口。相当多的中国人、法国人和意大利人来到这里定居。后来，这里有了电影产业。在二战中，这座城市生产战备物资，因此工人们涌入这里寻找工作。农场慢慢变成了郊区。如今洛杉矶是美国的第二大城市。

suburb *n.* 郊区；城外

20

A Visit to Olvera Street

In 1926 Christine Sterling took a walk through the plaza in the oldest part of Los Angeles. The area was *run-down* and *shabby*. On a small *lane* stood a few rooms of a *condemned* house. The lane was Olvera Street. It had been named for Agustin Olvera, who had once lived there. He was the first county judge of Los Angeles. The

走访欧维拉街

1926年，克里斯廷·斯特林散步穿过洛杉矶城最古老部分的广场。这个地方破败不堪。一条小路上仍然残存着几间破旧的房屋，它们已被定为不能住人的危房。这条小路就是欧维拉街。这条街以奥古斯丁·欧维拉命名，他是洛杉矶的第一位县法官，曾经居住在此。这所旧房子就是阿维拉泥砖房，过去是这个城市最好的房子之一，曾有市长住过此处。洛杉矶的诞生地变得如此破败不堪，斯特林觉得很难过。她开始

---

run-down *adj.* 破败的；失修的
lane *n.* 小路

shabby *adj.* 破旧的；破败的
condemn *v.* 宣告使用……不安全

old house was the Avila Adobe. It had been one of the finest houses in the city. The city's mayor had lived there. Sterling was sad that the birthplace of Los Angeles had become so run-down. She started a corporation to raise funds to fix it up. *The Los Angeles Times* told of the project. Many people gave money. The city drew the plans to fix the street. Prisoners did some of the work. Other people also gave their time and labor.

Today Olvera Street is a Mexican marketplace. It is lined with stores and wood *stalls*. Tourists come to shop for handmade pots, toys, clothes, art, and jewelry. Musicians stroll up and down the street playing instruments. Native peoples dance. One can eat Mexican food and visit the Avila Adobe. The street is part of a large state park. The park includes the plaza, or town square, and many *restored* buildings.

运营一个公司来募款修缮这条街。《洛杉矶时报》提及了这个项目，很多人开始捐钱。市政也做了规划修葺这条街。囚犯们做了其中的一部分工作，还有很多其他人付出了时间和劳力。

如今，欧维拉街是墨西哥市集。它的两侧商店和木制的摊位林立。旅游者来这里购买手工制作的罐子、玩具、衣物、艺术品和珠宝。音乐家们在街上巡回演出，弹奏各种乐器，本地人在此翩翩起舞。这里可以品尝墨西哥食物并参观阿维拉泥砖房。这条街还是一个相当大的州公园的一部分。整个公园包括广场(或称为城市广场)，以及很多重新修葺过的建筑物。

---

stall *n.* 货摊；摊位   restore *v.* 修复；整修

21

The Continental Army: America's First Army

By 1775 many American *colonists* wanted to be free of British rule. These *patriots* had gathered arms and formed troops. They could be ready to fight quickly, so they were called *Minutemen*. In New England, these groups formed armies to protect their *regions*. In the spring, the Second Continental Congress met.

大陆军：美国的第一支军队

到1775年的时候，很多英属北美殖民地的居民想从英国的统治下解放出来。这些爱国主义者已经集结了大量的武器，还组成了队伍。他们可以快速备战，投入战役，所以又称为"民兵"。在新英格兰，这些队伍整编成了若干军队保护各自的区域。1775年春天，第二届大陆会议召开，会上约翰·亚当斯认为整个殖民地需要一支庞大的军队来

---

colonist *n.* 殖民地定居者   patriot *n.* 爱国者
Minuteman *n.* 民兵；即召民兵   region *n.* 地区；区域

John Adams thought the colonies needed a *grand* army to defend themselves. Congress agreed to take on the expense of a united army. George Washington was chosen to lead the troops.

That summer Washington took charge of the Continental Army. There were about 17,000 soldiers. They were not well trained. Soldiers signed up for a few weeks and then went home. There were shortages of *gunpowder*, horses, and *uniforms*. Some people, including some members of Congress, did not support the army. They feared it would rule the country after the war. This made it hard for the army to get supplies. Washington did the best he could with what he had. Some soldiers wore parts of old uniforms. The rest wore their own clothes. *Badges* were worn to show rank.

The British soldiers were well trained. They had tents, food, guns,

---

进行自我防御。大会一致同意为联合军队提供军饷，并任命乔治·华盛顿为统帅。

同年夏天，华盛顿接管了大陆军，当时，大约有17 000个士兵。这些士兵没有受过很好的训练，他们临时入伍几周，然后再各自回家。大陆军缺少火药、战马和制服。有一部分人，包括国会的一些成员也不支持大陆军。这些人担心，战后大陆军会统治国家。这使得大陆军获得补给非常困难。华盛顿倾入了自己的全部精力和财力。有些士兵身穿旧制服，还有人穿着自己的衣服。士兵们佩戴徽章用以区分他们的军衔。

然而，英军却是训练有素，他们配有帐篷、食物、枪支和红色的制

---

grand *adj.* 宏大的；宏伟的
uniform *n.* 制服；校服

gunpowder *n.* 火药
badge *n.* 徽章；奖章

and red uniforms. The British also had funds to hire troops to fight with them. Some of these *mercenaries* were the German *Hessians*. Still, the Continental Army had some advantages. The colonists knew the land well. They could hide and launch surprise attacks. They could quickly call up more men. Most of all, they were fighting for their freedom.

In the fall of 1776, the British took over New York City. Washington's small army of three thousand men *retreated* across the Delaware River. The British thought they had won the war. In a bold move on Christmas Day, Washington and his men crossed the river at night. Their *password* was "Victory or Death!" They surprised the Hessian troops, who gave up. This did much to boost the morale of the army.

服。英国人还有专门的拨款来雇佣一些随军作战的队伍，其中就有德国的黑森雇佣军。不过，大陆军也有自己的优势：他们非常了解当地地形；他们可以隐蔽起来然后攻其不备；他们随时可以召集更多的人参战；最重要的是，他们是为自由而战。

1776年秋天，英军控制了纽约城。华盛顿率领一支只有3 000人的小部队撤退到德拉华河对岸。英国人认为他们赢得了战争。但在圣诞节这天，华盛顿采取了一次大胆的行动，他率领一些人夜渡德拉华河。他们的暗语是"胜利或者死亡！"。他们突袭了黑森雇佣军，迫使他们投降。这极大地鼓舞了整个军队的士气。

---

mercenary *n.* 雇佣兵
retreat *v.* 撤退；兵退

Hessian *n.* 黑森雇佣兵
password *n.* 暗语；暗号

By the winter of 1777, the army was in sad shape. The soldiers were camped at Valley Forge. They lacked tents and food. It was cold and some men did not have shoes. More than two thousand died. Baron von Steuben, a military leader from Prussia, joined them. He trained and *drilled* the troops. They became a strong fighting *force*. In 1778 France joined the colonies in the war. Their guns, soldiers, and ships helped the Continental Army win the war.

到了1777年冬天，大陆军已经溃不成形。士兵们在福吉谷安营扎寨，他们既缺帐篷又没有足够的食物。天气已经很冷，很多人都没有鞋子穿。2 000多名士兵死去。施托伊本男爵是一名从普鲁士来的军事领袖，他加入大陆军，训练这支军队，使它成为了一股强大的作战力量。1778年，法国加入这场殖民地的独立战争。法国人的枪支、士兵和战舰帮助大陆军赢得了战争的胜利。

drill *v.* 培训；训练

force *n.* 力量；部队

22

Who Were the Soldiers in the Continental Army?

The soldiers of the Continental Army were the rich and the poor. They were farmers, *blacksmiths*, merchants, and *woodsmen*. They were boys and men of all ages. Many had to learn how to carry, *load*, and shoot a *rifle*. Most knew nothing about fighting. A few were Native Americans. Some were African Americans,

大陆军的士兵都有谁?

大陆军的士兵有富人也有穷人。他们中有农民、铁匠、商人和樵夫,有男孩也有不同年龄段的成年男子。很多人必须学习如何携带、如何装填弹药和如何用步枪射击。而且,大多数人对战争一无所知。大陆军的士兵也有很少一部分是美洲土著人。还有一部分是获得自由或者仍是奴隶身份的非裔美洲人。有一个名叫彼得 · 塞勒姆的奴隶,他

---

blacksmith *n.* 铁匠
load *v.* 把……装入;装上

woodsman *n.* 樵夫;伐木工
rifle *n.* 步枪;来复枪

both free and *enslaved*. One enslaved man who fought was Peter Salem. He killed a British leader at the Battle of Bunker Hill. At one time, Congress did not allow enslaved persons in the army. Salem's owners freed him so he could stay in the army. Some women traveled with the army. They cooked and mended clothes. They nursed the sick and fought in *combat*.

These people came together to fight for one goal—freedom. Many endured hardships. "Long Bill" Scott was one of these freedom fighters. He was captured by the British in Boston. He escaped and *rejoined* the army in New York. Then he was captured in New York and escaped again. But "Long Bill" Scott was determined to fight for his country. When he rejoined the army, he brought his sons and some other men that he had *recruited*. He was wounded nine times. He had to sell his farm to pay his war expenses. He suffered through all of this to fight for freedom.

在邦克山战役中杀死了一名英国军官。那时，国会不允许被奴役的人待在军队里。彼得的主人让他成为自由身，使得他能继续待在军队里。也有一些妇女跟随军队，煮饭和缝补衣物，她们还照看生病的士兵，有时候也参战。

参加大陆军的人都是为了一个共同的目标——自由而战。很多人忍受了各种艰难困苦。"老家伙"斯科特是这些自由斗士中的一员。他曾在波士顿被英军俘虏，而后逃跑，然后在纽约重新加入军队。在纽约，他又一次被捕，而后再逃脱。但是斯科特坚定地为自己的国家而战。当他又一次入伍时，他带来了自己的儿子和他招募的其他人。他曾九次受伤，还把自己的农场卖掉用以支付战争所需的费用。他所做的一切都是为自由而战斗。

---

enslave *v.* 使成为奴隶；奴役　　　　combat *n.* 战斗；打仗
rejoin *v.* 重新加入　　　　　　　　recruit *v.* 招募；征募

23

The Nile River: Lifeblood of Ancient Egypt

The Nile is the world's longest river. It starts in the mountains of East Africa. It flows through the *barren* desert and ends in the *Mediterranean* Sea. Along its banks, the first great African *civilization* grew. This was ancient Egypt. By 5000 b.c., people were living on the Nile's *floodplain*. This lowland on both sides of the river

尼罗河：古埃及的生命根源

尼罗河是世界上最长的河流，发源于非洲东部的山脉。它流经贫瘠的沙漠之地，最后注入地中海。沿着尼罗河两岸，最早的伟大非洲文明发展起来，这就是古埃及文明。到公元前5000年的时候，人们居住在尼罗河的泛滥平原即"河漫滩"上。河流两岸的低地每年发一次

---

barren *adj.* 贫瘠的；不毛的　　　　Mediterranean *adj.* 地中海的
civilization *n.* 文明；社会文明　　　floodplain *n.* 洪泛区；漫滩

floods once a year. Each spring, *snowmelt* in the mountains sends a rush of water down the river. The fast water picks up *silt*, which is bits of soil and plant matter. In the desert, the Nile overflows its banks. When the water *recedes*, it leaves a layer of silt. This rich new *topsoil* is good for growing crops. When the crops are growing, the land near the river looks like a green ribbon running through the brown desert. The long Nile valley is only five miles wide in some places.

The ancient people planted their seeds in the mud. They grew wheat, barley, flax, beans, chickpeas, onions, and other vegetables. They also grew trees that produced fruit, such as figs and dates. Because the climate is warm, there is a long growing season. Two or three crops could be grown each year. The people built canals

---

洪水。每年春天，从山上融化的雪水奔流而下汇入尼罗河水，这股湍急的水流一路夹带的淤泥，就是丰富的土壤和植物残骸。在沙漠地区，尼罗河水溢出两岸。每当水流退去，就留下一层淤泥。这层富含养分的新鲜表土有利于庄稼的生长。庄稼繁茂生长时，河水附近的土地就像是棕黄沙漠里的一条绿色缎带。在一些地方，长长的尼罗河的河谷只有五英里宽。

古埃及人在泥土里播种。他们种植小麦、大麦、亚麻、豆类、鹰嘴豆、洋葱以及其他的蔬菜。他们还种植果树，例如无花果树和枣树。因为气候温暖，这里的植物生长季很长。每年作物都能两收或者三收。当时的

---

snowmelt *n.* 雪融水；解冻水
recede *v.* 逐渐远离；后退

silt *n.* 泥沙；淤泥
topsoil *n.* 表土；表土层

and *basins* that filled with water when the river flooded. They used this water on the crops for the rest of the year. A flood that had less water than normal meant there would be fewer crops that year.

Besides growing crops, the ancient people of the Nile gathered wild fruits, seeds, and roots near the river. They fished the river for *catfish*, *perch*, and other kinds of fish. Animals—such as *gazelles*, hyenas, and birds—lived on the river's banks. The people hunted these animals for food. They tamed other animals and kept them as livestock. They raised cattle and flocks of geese. From these animals, they got meat, eggs, and fat.

The Nile was more than a source of food to the ancient Egyptians. They dried and bundled the reeds that grew by the water. They coated the reeds with straw and mud and used them to build homes.

人修建了运河和水池，当河流涨水它们就会满溢，在雨季之外的其他时节，就用这些水浇灌庄稼。如果某次水量不比常年，那就意味着当年庄稼会减产。

古埃及人除了种庄稼外，还在尼罗河附近采摘野果、种子和根菜类植物。他们在河里捕鱼：捕鲶鱼、河鲈和其他各种鱼。羚羊、鬣狗和鸟类等动物也都生活在河的两岸，人们捕猎动物作为食物。古埃及人还驯化了一些动物将其作为家畜。他们饲养牛群和成群的鹅，并取用它们身上的肉、蛋和油脂。

对古埃及人来说，尼罗河不仅仅是食物的来源。他们晒干河水附近生

---

basin *n.* 船坞；水池
perch *n.* 鲈鱼；河鲈

catfish *n.* 鲶鱼；鲇
gazelle *n.* 羚羊

They made roofs for their homes from the *fronds* of *palm* trees that grew by the water. They built their first *monuments* to their gods from sun-dried mud bricks. They traveled on the river in boats made from *reeds* and wood.

长的芦苇并把它们扎好，然后把稻草和泥覆盖在这些芦苇之上，用于搭建房屋，房子的屋顶用河边的棕榈树叶做成。此外，他们还用太阳晒干的泥砖建造了他们的首个敬神的纪念碑。古埃及人乘着小船在尼罗河里穿行，这些船由芦苇和木头制成。

frond *n.* （尤指棕榈类或蕨类的）叶   palm *n.* 棕榈树
monument *n.* 纪念碑；历史遗迹   reed *n.* 芦苇

24

The Boats of Ancient Egypt

The ancient Egyptians traveled most often by boat. The Nile River became a *bustling* freeway of boats, from simple rafts to beautiful boats.

Rafts and small boats were made of *papyrus* reeds. The ambatch was a small *craft* shaped like a canoe. To make an ambatch, a person first tied two bundles of

古埃及人的船只

古埃及人主要靠船只出行。当时尼罗河成了一条熙熙攘攘的航线，上面不但有简易木筏，也有漂亮的船。

木筏和小船都是用纸莎草制成。阿姆拜持划艇是一种形似独木舟的船。要造一条这样的划艇，首先要把两捆芦苇在船两端系住，然后居中把

---

bustling *adj.* 繁忙的；熙熙攘攘的   papyrus *n.* 纸莎草
craft *n.* 小船；船

reeds together at the ends. Then the reeds were parted in the middle to form the sides and the bottom of the boat. Finally, a reed *mat* was placed in the boat for a floor. A person would use a paddle to move the boat.

Large boats were made from wood. Boats called *merchantmen* carried trade goods. These boats had sails, but they were also rowed by many people. Large ships went down the Nile to the Mediterranean Sea.

Barges were large wooden boats pulled by smaller boats. Enslaved people rowed the smaller boats. Some barges carried animals. Others carried the blocks of stone used to build the *pyramids*. Kings rode on royal barges that were painted to tell a story. The king sat

---

这些芦苇分开做船的侧面和底部。最后，在做好的船底铺上一层芦苇席子。用浆划水，小船就能行进了。

大一点儿的船用木头来造。称为"商船"的船只用来运输贸易商品，这种船有帆，但也需要很多人来划。大型船只都沿着尼罗河而下驶到地中海。

驳船是靠若干小船牵引的一种大型木船，由奴隶们来划动那些小船。一些驳船运载动物，还有一些运载用来建造金字塔的成批的石头。埃及法老们乘坐皇家驳船，坐在华盖下，船体上绘有图案，这些图案通常讲述着某个故事。据说埃及女王克里奥帕特拉有一艘带有若干私人房间的皇家驳

---

mat *n.* 小地毯；垫子
barge *n.* 驳船

merchantman *n.* 商船；商人
pyramid *n.* 金字塔

under a cloth cover. It is thought that Queen Cleopatra had a royal barge with private rooms. *Funeral* barges carried dead kings to their tombs. *Solar* barges were often buried near the kings. People thought the kings could use these boats in the *afterlife*.

船。葬礼专用驳船会载着法老的遗体驶向他们的陵墓。太阳船经常埋在已故法老的陵墓附近。那时，人们认为法老死后会用到这些船。

funeral *n.* 葬礼；丧礼　　　　　　　　　　solar *adj.* 太阳的；太阳能的
afterlife *n.* 死后（灵魂）的生活；来生

25

What Is an *Entrepreneur*?

Entrepreneurs are people who start and run their own businesses. They want to be in control of their own time and *fortune*. They take the risk of investing in a business. If it succeeds, they make a profit. If it fails, they take the loss. Entrepreneurs work in a free *enterprise* system. This means that people can own resources such as

对企业家的界定

企业家是指那些自己创办并经营自己企业的人。他们希望掌控自己的时间和财富，也承担投资风险。他们享受成功带来的财富，同时也承受失败带来的损失。企业家工作在自由的企业制度中，这意

---

entrepreneur *n.* 创业者；企业家　　　　　　　fortune *n.* 财富；命运
enterprise *n.* 公司；企业经营

land, computers, and buildings. They can use these to make goods or offer services. A business must follow certain laws. However, a business owner has the freedom to make most decisions.

How does a person know what kind of business to start? An entrepreneur sees a need that is not being filled. This is called an "opportunity *niche*". For example, many people in a small town have pets. The closest place to leave the pets while on vacation is 50 miles away. A pet-sitting service would fill this niche.

Entrepreneurs often invent new things. In the 1940s, George de Mestral took his dog for a walk. His pants picked up plant *burrs*. He looked at the burrs under a microscope. They had tiny hooks that stuck to the *loops* of the pants *fabric*. He thought of making a hook-

---

味着他们能够拥有土地、电脑和房屋等资源，并利用这些资源生产商品或者提供服务。企业经营必须遵循一定的法则。不过，企业法人有自己作大部分决策的自由。

那么一个人怎么才能知道从哪种行业起步呢？企业家会寻找需求，也就是所谓的"商机"。举例来说，小镇里的很多人都养宠物，但是人们出去度假时需要寄养宠物，最近的地方也在50英里外，那么，宠物寄养服务就是这里的商机。

创业者也会自己发明新的东西。20世纪40年代的时候，乔治·德·梅斯特拉尔在一次遛狗后，长裤上沾上了一些植物的小刺果。他用显微镜观察这些小刺果，发现上面有细小的钩能够挂在长裤布料的毛圈上，便想

---

niche *n.* 商机；利基　　　　　　burr *n.* （某些植物）带芒刺的小果实
loop *n.* 环形；圆圈　　　　　　fabric *n.* 织物；布料

and-loop *fastener*. Thus, Velcro was born.

Entrepreneurs may not have the funds to start a business. But that does not stop them. They may borrow money from a bank. They may convince others to invest in their ideas for a share of the profits. In New York, teen Jeffrey Rodriguez learned to paint with an *airbrush*. This is a tool that uses air to *spray* paint on a surface. His first tools were borrowed from his Boy Scout leader. His dad let him use a *storefront* that the family owned. Rodriguez and a partner, John Serrano, started a custom art business. They called it Latin Artist. Still, they needed money. Rodriguez learned of a group that gave grants to businesses that stressed community service. A grant is money that does not have to be paid back. Rodriguez and his partner won a grant. Latin Artist gives young people free art lessons.

到制造一种钩和毛圈搭扣。于是，"维可牢"诞生了。

　　企业家可能会没有启动企业的资金，但这并不能成为他们事业发展的障碍。他们可以从银行贷款，也可以说服他人为他们的想法投资并共分利润。在纽约，十几岁的杰弗里·罗德里格斯学会了用喷枪作画，喷枪是靠空气压力把颜料喷到物体表面上的一种工具。他第一次使用的喷枪是借用他的童子军首领的，另外，他爸爸允许他使用家里的一处店面。于是，罗德里格斯和他的合伙人约翰·塞拉诺开始了订制艺术画的事业，起名为"拉丁艺术家"。可他们还是缺少资金。罗德里格斯了解到有一个组织专为那些旨在为社区服务的企业提供资金援助，援助金无须偿还。罗德里格

---

fastener　*n.* 拉链；扣件　　　　　　　airbrush　*n.* 气笔；喷枪
spray　*v.* 喷；喷洒　　　　　　　　　storefront　*n.* 商店门面；店面

The grant was used to fix up their workshop.

Once a business is running, entrepreneurs can change *course* as they go. They can come back and try again after a *loss*. Some start one business after another. They apply what they learn to each new *venture*.

斯和他的合作者争取到了这笔援助金。"拉丁艺术家"为年轻人提供免费的艺术课，援助金就用来解决工作坊所需的资金。

一旦企业运作起来，企业家可以在经营中改变方向，也可以失败后从头再来。有些企业家创办一个又一个的企业，他们把自己学到的东西运用到新的企业运营中。

---

course *n.* 方向；方针　　　　　　　　　　　loss *n.* 损失；失败
venture *n.* 企业；经营项目

26

Steps for Starting a Business—for Young People

Step one: Decide what kind of business to start. A person who likes to be outside might *mow lawns*. A teen who *baby-sits* might start a day camp for children.

Step two: Make sure there is a need for the business. Neighbors who dislike lawn *chores* might pay to have them done.

创业的步骤——致年轻人

第一步：决定从哪种生意做起。一个喜欢在户外待着的人可以做修剪草坪的生意。一个做过临时保姆的青少年可以为孩子们开办日间夏令营。

第二步：确保要做的生意有需求。不喜欢自己修剪草坪的街区居民很

---

mow *v.* 割；修剪
baby-sit *v.* 当临时保姆

lawn *n.* 草坪；草地
chore *n.* 日常事务；例行工作

Mothers of small children might pay to send them to camp.

Step three: Answer the following question. How can the new business be better than businesses that are already out there? A new lawn care service might cut grass free every fourth time. A day camp for children might teach *crafts*.

Step four: Get the needed resources. A lawn care service needs a mower and other tools. A camp needs snacks, craft supplies, and a *sheltered*, *shady* space. It may need an indoor space too. Some resources may have to be purchased. An entrepreneur might borrow money to buy them.

Step five: Advertise. Give out *flyers* or place an ad in a local paper.

Step six: Do what is promised in the ads. People will go back often to a business they can rely on.

可能会付钱请人修剪草坪。小孩的母亲们可能会付钱把孩子送进夏令营。

第三步：回答以下问题：新生意如何比现有的生意有优势？新的照料草坪的服务可以在三次服务后免费赠送一次剪草服务。日间夏令营可以给孩子们上手工课。

第四步：准备所需备品。照料草坪服务会需要割草机和其他的工具。夏令营需要零食、手工工具和一个能避雨遮阳的地方，或许还需要一个室内场所。创业者有时需要借钱购置一些备品。

第五步：广告。发放广告传单或者在当地报纸上登广告。

第六步：一定信守广告中的承诺。取得信誉，赢得生意的回头客。

---

craft *n.* 手艺；工艺
shady *adj.* 背阴的；阴凉的

sheltered *adj.* 遮蔽的；受庇护的
flyer *n.* 传单

Step seven: *Expand* the business. When the money comes in, put some of it back into the business. This might mean purchasing better equipment. It could mean hiring workers to take on more customers.

第七步：扩大经营。有钱赚的时候，要把一部分资金再投到生意中。这可能意味着购买更好的设备，也可能要雇员工来照顾更多的顾客。

---

expand *v.* 扩大；扩展

27

The Authority of the Kings and Queens of England

The United Kingdom (UK) of Great Britain and Northern Ireland is a *constitutional monarchy*. This means that a monarch (king or queen) is the head of state. His or her powers are limited by a constitution. These are laws and customs that serve as a *framework* for government. Laws are made by *Parliament*, which is made

英国国王和女王的权力

大不列颠及北爱尔兰联合王国是君主立宪制。君主（国王或者女王）是整个国家的元首，同时，国王或者女王的权力又受到宪法制约。宪法所规定的内容是政府决策的基本原则。议会立法，它由上议

---

constitutional *adj.* 宪法的
framework *n.* 观点；准则

monarchy *n.* 君主制；君主国
Parliament *n.* （英国）议会

up of the House of Lords and the House of Commons. The members of the House of Lords are *peers* (nobles) and officials of the Church of England. The members of the House of Commons are elected, and they are paid. Members of Parliament have the real power to govern. The king or queen can advise Parliament and can name new peers.

In the sixth century, the first kings of England were *warlords*. They seized land by force and passed it down to their *heirs*. They led warriors who fought to keep the land. The warriors were the *barons*, or lords. For their service, the king gave them land and wealth. To get wealth, a king taxed the people. These first kings had the power to solve disputes. They could fine and punish people. They made the laws.

院和下议院组成。上议院议员由隶属英国国教的贵族和官员组成。下议院议员由选举产生，而且有工资收入。议会的议员具有真正的统治权。国王或女王可以向议会提出建议，还可以提名新的贵族。

六世纪时，英格兰最初的几个国王可谓是好战的君王。他们武力攫取土地并传给自己的继承人。国王手下有一批善战的勇士，他们均有男爵或勋爵头衔，勇士们四处征战保卫土地。国王论功行赏，赐给他们土地和财富。为了获得财富，国王向民众征收赋税。起初的国王有权力解决纷争，他们有权处罚和惩戒人民，法律全由他们制定。

peer *n.* （英国）贵族成员
heir *n.* 继承人；承袭者

warlord *n.* 军阀；军阀式领袖
baron *n.* 男爵

Parliament began as a group of lords. Their job was to advise the monarch. Later the lords fought with the kings and queens for power. In the thirteenth century, the lords forced King John to sign *the Magna Carta*. It stated that upper-class people had certain rights. For example, they could not be put in jail without a *trial*. It held that even the king must obey the law. Years later the barons forced the king to have a permanent *council* of barons. Baron Simon de Montfort called some of his knights to attend one meeting. They were commoners. From then on, *commoners* took part in Parliament.

In the fourteenth century, the king could not make new taxes without Parliament's consent. Parliament split into the House of Lords and the House of Commons. In the next century, the House of Commons gained the same powers as the House of Lords.

议会最初由贵族组成，其职责就是向君主进谏。后来，这些贵族为获取权力开始同国王和女王斗争。13世纪时，贵族们强迫约翰国王签署了《大宪章》。宪章规定上层阶级拥有一定的权利。比如，未经审讯不得把上层阶级送入监狱。宪章还规定国王也必须遵守法律。若干年后，男爵们强迫国王同意成立贵族常设理事会。西蒙·德·蒙特福特男爵召集他的骑士们出席了会议，他们都是平民。从那时起，平民加入了议会。

14世纪时，不经议会同意国王不得征收新税。议会开始分为上议院和下议院。到了15世纪，下议院获得了和上议院同样的权力。

Magna Carta 大宪章
council *n.* 委员会；政务委员会

trial *n.* 审讯；审理
commoner *n.* 平民

A war between Parliament and Charles I was fought in the seventeenth century. The king lost his *throne*. After the war, *the Bill of Rights* was written. It gave Parliament more power than the king or queen. Today the queen has little power. She often attends ceremonies, and she is respected by the people as a symbol of their country.

17世纪时，查尔斯一世和议会交战，他丢了王位。战后，《权利法案》出台，它赋予议会比国王和女王更大的权力。当今女王几乎没有什么权力，她经常出席庆典，作为国家的象征受到人民的尊敬。

---

throne *n.* 王位；王权

28

In the Time of Queen Elizabeth I

In 1559 Elizabeth I was *crowned* Queen of England. She was young, and she faced problems. England was poor. There was the threat of war with Spain. At home, there was *unrest*. English citizens *clashed* over religion.

One of Elizabeth's first acts was to make the Church of England the state church.

女王伊丽莎白一世时期

1559 年伊丽莎白一世加冕为英格兰女王。当时，年轻的女王面临很多问题：国家贫困，又面对与西班牙的交战；国内也不得安宁，因宗教分歧，民众间冲突时有发生。

伊丽莎白最初的行动之一就是把英国圣公会确立为国家教会，接下来她尽力使英格兰远离战争。当时的西班牙富庶，而且还在"新大陆"拥有领土。于是，伊丽莎白派遣船员掠夺西班牙的船队。每当西班牙的船队从新大陆返航，英国人就会对他们进行抢劫。这不仅给英国带来了财富，还

---

crown *v.* 为……加冕

clash *v.* 差异；迥然不同

unrest *n.* 动荡；动乱

She then worked to keep England out of war. Spain was rich, and it had lands in the New World. Elizabeth sent sailors to *pirate* Spanish ships. As Spain's ships sailed from the New World, the English robbed them. This brought wealth to England. It put off war with Spain, as Spain had to have money to *wage* war. Later Spain sent its ships to attack England. The English ships defeated them.

Elizabeth *reigned* until her death in 1603. She made England rich and strong. Her reign was a time of world discovery. She sent the first English settlers to the New World. The colonies gave Britain greater power in the world. Elizabeth's reign was a time of rebirth of the arts. Literature and art *flourished*. The era was called the Renaissance. It began in Italy and spread to England. Elizabeth's court was a place where writers, musicians, and scholars worked. William Shakespeare wrote his plays at this time. Elizabeth's reign is called the Golden Age of English history.

延缓了和西班牙的战争，因为西班牙不得不为发动战争准备钱财。后来，西班牙派出舰队袭击英格兰，被英格兰舰队击败。

伊丽莎白的统治持续到1603年，直到她去世。她成就了英格兰的富庶和强大。她的统治时期也是探索世界的时期。她派出第一批英国人去新大陆定居。殖民地使得英国在世界上更加强大。伊丽莎白统治时期也是艺术重新崛起的时期，文学和艺术遍地开花，这一时期史称为"文艺复兴"。文艺复兴始于意大利，蔓延到英格兰。伊丽莎白的宫廷也是作家、音乐家和学者们发挥才能的地方。威廉·莎士比亚在这一时期创作出他的不朽之作。伊丽莎白时期在英国历史上亦称为"黄金时代"。

---

pirate *v.* 掠夺；盗用
reign *v.* 统治；当政

wage *v.* 开始；发动（战争等）
flourish *v.* 繁荣；兴旺

29

The Inuit: People of the Cold

The Inuit live in the cold climates of the North. They live near the coasts of Greenland, North Siberia, and the Arctic. This area includes parts of Canada and Alaska. Inuit means "the people". Today many Inuit live in western-style houses. They wear *ready-made* clothes and buy food

因纽特人：生活在寒冷中的人

因纽特人生活在北部寒冷的气候环境之中。他们居住在格陵兰岛、北西伯利亚以及北极圈附近的海岸边。这一地带包括加拿大和阿拉斯加的一部分。"因纽特"意思是"人们"。如今，很多因纽特

---

ready-made *adj.* 现成的；做好的

at grocery stores. However, their traditional way of life reflects the climate in which they have lived since early times.

In the Arctic, the treeless ground stays frozen year round. Summers are short, and the sun shines day and night. The temperature may rise to 50 degrees. Winters are long. The sun does not shine for months. Temperatures are subzero. There are snowstorms and strong winds. In the past, the Inuit dressed in layers of fur clothes to keep warm. The women used *caribou sinew* as thread, and they sewed with bone needles. They made watertight *parkas* from *seal* or walrus intestines.

The men hunted for the family's food. Families ate fish, seals, whales, polar bears, hares, foxes, and sea birds. To hunt, the Inuit traveled over the ice and snow on dog sleds. The sleds had

---

人居住的房子具有西式建筑风格，他们穿现成的衣服，还在杂货店买食品。不过，他们传统的生活方式正是他们所处的气候环境的写照，从很久以前他们生存的气候环境就如此。

在北极圈内，光溜溜的地面整年都冰冻着。夏季很短，有极昼，温度会高达50摄氏度。冬季漫长，有长达几个月的极夜，温度在零度以下，并且有暴风雪和强风天气。过去，为了取暖，因纽特人的衣服由几层毛皮制成，女人们用骨头做成的针和北美驯鹿的腱制成的线来缝制衣服，还用海豹和海象的肠子来做防水的毛皮外套。

男人们打猎养家。鱼、海豹、鲸鱼、北极熊、野兔、狐狸和海鸟都是

---

caribou *n.* 北美驯鹿
parka *n.* 风雪外套

sinew *n.* 肌腱
seal *n.* 海豹

whalebone runners. They were pulled by native dogs. Hunters used *harpoons* of bone or walrus *tusk* to spear their *prey*. They might wait for hours by an ice hole for a walrus to come up for air. They also hunted by boat. One boat, a *kayak*, is a canoe-like craft covered with sealskin. One person sits in the boat, and the skin is laced up around him. Another boat is called a umiak. It is an open boat made for more than one person. Hunters teamed up to hunt walruses or whales.

Families lived in igloos built by the men. The word igloo means "house". A winter house was a hut usually made of sod or stone. The frame for the roof was made of whalebone. The roof was covered with sod, moss, or walrus hides. Inside the igloo, the Inuit slept on a platform of furs. Heat and light came from stone lamps that

他们的食物。因纽特人坐着狗拉雪橇在冰雪上穿行打猎，这些雪橇的轮子由鲸鱼骨头做成，当地的狗拉着雪橇前行。猎手们用骨制鱼叉或者海象牙制成的鱼叉刺向猎物。他们可以在海象出来呼吸的冰洞边一等数小时。他们也坐船打猎。爱斯基摩小艇是一种形似独木舟的手工制船，上面铺着海豹皮。船上坐一个人，把海豹皮围在身上系住。另一种船是皮筏，是一种能坐不只一人的敞篷船。猎手们结队去捕猎海象或者鲸鱼。

因纽特家庭居住在男人们建造的冰屋"伊格鲁"中。这个词就是"房子"的意思。冬季的房子通常是用草皮和石头建造的小屋，屋顶的框架由鲸鱼骨头构成。屋顶盖着草皮，苔藓或者是海象皮。小屋里面，因纽特人

harpoon *n.* 渔叉；渔猎标枪

prey *n.* 猎物

tusk *n.* 长牙

kayak *n.* 爱斯基摩小艇

burned animal fat. Fuel was not often used for cooking. Most meat was eaten raw. In the spring, melting snow would *collapse* the roof. The men would build a new house somewhere else the next winter. Domes built of snow blocks were used as shelter on long trips. In the summer, the people lived in tents made of *hides*.

睡在一个铺满毛皮的台上。取暖和采光都来自石头灯，里面燃着动物油脂。他们不常用燃料做饭，多数肉都是生吃的。春季的时候，融化的雪可能会把屋顶弄塌。这样，第二年冬天男人们会在另一个地方再建一个房子。雪块造的圆屋顶是长途出行在外的避风港。夏季，因纽特人住在兽皮做的帐篷里。

collapse *v.* 倒塌；瓦解

hide *n.* 皮；毛皮

30

Inuit Art

The Inuit way of life is expressed in their art. For hundreds of years, the Inuit made art from things they had at hand such as *ivory*. Ivory comes from walrus tusks or whale teeth. They carved the ivory into *figures* of people and animals. They shaped it into useful things such as *knobs* and tools. Their carvings had *decorative*

因纽特艺术

因纽特人的生活方式表现在他们的艺术之中。千百年来，因纽特人一直用他们手边的物品创造艺术品，比如象牙制品，是用海象的牙或者鲸鱼的牙齿做的。他们把象牙雕刻成人物和动物的形象，做成诸如球状把手和工具等有用的物品。他们的雕刻物都有装饰设计。象牙雕刻艺术被称为"解闷手工"。因纽特人也用鹿角、麝牛角和石头进行雕刻。他们还用象牙和石头制作珠宝，用鲸鱼骨和浮木雕刻面具。一些面具

---

ivory *n.* 象牙；象牙制品
knob *n.* 球形把手

figure *n.* 雕像；塑像
decorative *adj.* 装饰性的

designs. The art of carving on ivory is called *scrimshaw*. The Inuit also carved *antlers*, *musk ox* horn, and stone. They used ivory and bone to make jewelry. They used whalebone or *driftwood* to carve masks. Some masks were very small, and others were huge.

The Inuit have made dolls for at least 1,000 years. Heads were made of leather or soapstone. Fur was used for hair. Dolls were dressed in clothes of fur and skins. By cutting and sewing dolls, Inuit girls learned skills they would use later to make waterproof clothing. Some dolls were so small they could be carried in a mitten.

When the first Europeans came, the Inuit used carvings for trade. The women made fur clothes to trade.

Today Inuit artists still make carvings, jewelry, dolls, and clothes. Some clothing is made from wool. Their art now includes painting, pottery, and cloth pictures. Inuit art reflects both past and present Inuit life.

非常小，另外一些则很大。

因纽特人做玩偶最少有1 000年了。玩偶的头是羽毛和滑石做的，头发是毛做的。玩偶们身着毛皮做成的衣服。通过为玩偶剪裁和缝制衣服，因纽特女孩们学会了日后制作防水衣服的技巧。有些玩偶小到可以装在连指手套里。

第一批欧洲人到来后，因纽特人用雕刻物进行交易，女人们制作的毛皮衣服也拿来交易。

现在因纽特艺术家仍然制作雕刻品、珠宝、玩偶和衣服。有些衣服是羊毛做的。他们的艺术品现在包括了绘画、陶瓷和布画。因纽特艺术既反映了过去因纽特人的生活，也反映了现在他们的生活。

---

scrimshaw *n.* 解闷手工　　　　　　　antler *n.* 鹿角
musk ox 麝牛　　　　　　　　　　　driftwood *n.* 浮木；漂流木

31

The First Voyage of Columbus

Christopher Columbus was an Italian explorer in the fifteenth century. At that time, people did not think of the world the way they do today. Many people thought the world was *flat*. Exploring new lands took courage. Explorers had to be *willing* to go into the unknown. Many people believed sea *monsters* living in the ocean

哥伦布的首次航海

克里斯托弗·哥伦布是15世纪意大利的探险家。那个时候，人们对世界的看法和如今不同。很多人都认为地球是平的。探索新大陆需要勇气。探险家们必须要心甘情愿地走进未知世界。很多人相信航

---

flat *adj.* 平坦的；水平的   willing *adj.* 愿意的；自愿的
monster *n.* 怪物；怪兽

would attack a ship. Some were afraid they would fall off the edge of the earth if they traveled too far.

Columbus thought he could find a way to the Indies by sailing west. This would be a good trade route. Columbus tried to get help from the king of Portugal. The king said no. So Columbus went to King Ferdinand and Queen Isabella of Spain. Spain wanted new land to add to its empire. With a better trade route, Spain would be able to buy things such as *spices* and silk. Even so, it took Columbus almost seven years to convince the king and queen. Finally they said yes. Columbus could begin his voyage.

He *assembled* three ships. They were the Niña, the Pinta, and the Santa Maria. He recruited a *crew* of about 85 men. On August 3, 1492, he sailed west from Palos, Spain. Columbus sailed on

---

行的船只会遭到海怪袭击。有些人还担心如果他们走得太远，可能会从地球的边缘掉下去。

哥伦布却认为向西航行能到达东印度群岛，而且这会是个极好的贸易路线。他试图寻求葡萄牙国王的帮助，但遭到拒绝。于是他又去找了西班牙的费迪南德国王和伊莎贝拉女王。当时，西班牙想得到新大陆来扩张自己的领土。如果有更好的贸易路线，西班牙就能够买到诸如香料和蚕丝这类的东西。即便如此，哥伦布还是用了几乎七年的时间才说服了西班牙国王和女王。最后，他们终于同意了。这样，哥伦布能够开始他的航海了。

哥伦布集结了三艘船：尼娜号、平塔号和圣玛利亚号，招募了大约

---

spice *n.* 香料

crew *n.* 全体船员；全体工作人员

assemble *v.* 聚集；集合

the Santa Maria. It was the largest of the three ships. On the trip, the ships stopped for supplies in the Canary Islands. Then they continued southwest.

The journey was very hard. The work on the ships was *exhausting*. At that time, ships used for exploration had to carry enough supplies for very long periods of time. No one knew how long a ship might have to be out in the open sea. Food often *spoiled*. Water was in short supply.

Because no one could be sure Columbus would find what he was looking for, members of the crew were afraid. After several weeks at sea, they wanted to turn back. Columbus refused. Some say there was talk of *mutiny*. A number of the men were sick. They couldn't see land. Columbus asked the crew to wait three more days. The

---

85名船员。1492年8月3日，他从西班牙的帕洛斯港口出发，向西航行。哥伦布在圣玛利亚号船上，它是三艘船里面最大的一艘。航行途中，船队在加那利群岛停泊进行补给。然后，继续向西南行进。

航海旅途非常险恶，船上的工作让人精疲力竭。那时候，探险船上不得不载着足够长期使用的补给，因为没人知道多久船才可能驶出一片浩瀚的海域。船上食物常常坏掉，淡水缺乏。

没人确信哥伦布能够发现他一直在寻找的东西，船员们也都很害怕。在海上航行几周后，船员们就产生了返航的想法，但哥伦布不同意。有传言，当时船员讨论过叛乱。一部分船员病了，四处不见陆地。哥伦布要求

---

exhausting *adj.* 使人疲惫不堪的
mutiny *n.* 哗变；暴动

spoil *v.* 变坏；变质

next day they saw a *flock* of birds. This meant land must be close by. Soon they saw dolphins and a tree *branch*. On October 12, 1492, the ships landed on an island in the Bahamas. Columbus, however, thought he had found an island off the coast of Asia. Columbus named the island San Salvador.

船员们再多待三天。次日他们看到了鸟群，这意味着陆地就在附近。不久，他们看到了海豚和树枝。1492年10月12日，船队停泊在巴哈马群岛的一个岛屿上。但是，哥伦布认为他找到的是亚洲海岸，他把这个岛命名为圣萨尔瓦多。

---

flock *n.* （羊或鸟）群   branch *n.* 树枝

32

The Niña, the Pinta, and the Santa Maria

Christopher Columbus sailed to the New World with three ships. These ships were the Niña, the Pinta, and the Santa Maria. Each ship was slightly different. Life on all three ships was hard. Food was *scarce* and frequently spoiled.

The Niña was a *caravel*. Caravels were

尼娜号、平塔号和圣玛利亚号

哥伦布驾驶三艘船驶向美洲，这三艘船分别是尼娜号、平塔号和圣玛利亚号，每艘船都略有不同。船上的生活十分艰难，食物短缺且经常变质。

尼娜号属轻快型帆船。轻快帆船为小型帆船，它们能在宽阔的海域中

---

scarce *adj.* 缺乏的；不足的　　　　　caravel *n.* 轻快帆船；小型帆船

small sailing ships. They were designed to travel in the wind on the open ocean. They could not carry much *cargo*. Explorers often used caravels. The Niña was the smallest and fastest of the three ships. The Niña was Columbus's favorite ship. He returned to Spain aboard her. He also used her for many later trips.

The Pinta was a caravel too. The Pinta was slightly larger and slower than the Niña. The Pinta returned to Spain with Columbus's crew. But no one is sure what happened to the Pinta after that. Some say that she made a few trips to the Caribbean before sinking in a storm.

The Santa Maria was the *fleet*'s *flagship*. It was a nao, which was made to carry cargo. This kind of ship was slow. It was not meant for explorers. The Santa Maria was the largest ship, so Columbus chose to captain that ship on his first journey. The ship ran aground in the New World and sank.

乘风破浪，不能装载太多的货物，是开拓者经常使用的船型。尼娜号在这三艘船中体积最小，速度最快，也是哥伦布最喜欢的船。他返回西班牙就是驾驶的尼娜号，而且后来的多次航行也是驾驶的尼娜号。

平塔号也是一艘轻快帆船，比尼娜号大一点，也慢一点。平塔号也随着哥伦布的船队返回了西班牙，但是没有人能确切地说出它的最后结局。有人说平塔号去了几次加勒比海，之后就在风暴中沉没了。

圣玛利亚号是船队中的旗舰，用来装载货物，航行速度很慢。其实，对探险者来说这种船并不适合。但圣玛利亚号是最大的船，所以哥伦布选择它在首航中领航。这艘船在新大陆搁浅并且沉没。

---

cargo *n.* （船或飞机装载的）货物　　　　　　　　　　　fleet *n.* 舰队
flagship *n.* 旗舰；王牌

33

Becoming a History Teacher

History is a record of the people and events of the past. The study of history shows how the past has shaped today's world. History is a basic part of everyone's schooling. Teachers in this field have a *firm grasp* of social studies. They have an in-depth knowledge of the human past. They usually like to study maps and

如何成为一名历史教师

历史是对过去的人物和事件的记录。历史的研究揭示了过去如何演变成了今天的世界。历史是每个人学校教育的一个基本部分。历史教师往往精通社会研究，深入了解人类的过去。他们通常喜欢研

---

firm *adj.* 牢固的；掌握的   grasp *n.* 理解；领会

read stories about people's lives.

To be a history teacher, a person must have training and skills. Someone who wants to teach must have a college *degree*. A training program is useful as well. Teachers must be able to communicate well. They must know how to *present* information to their students. Teachers must know how to manage a classroom. They need to enjoy working with young people.

Students who want to be history teachers can begin to *gain* the skills they need in high school. They can take social studies courses. They can *tutor* classmates. They can work with young children. Learning about social studies and knowing how to work with others can prepare students for their college studies.

People who want to teach history must earn college degrees in

---

究人类图谱，阅读历史故事。

历史老师必须经过相应的培训并掌握相关技能。要成为一名教师，首先必须获得学士学位，同样接受培训也很有帮助。教师要有很好的沟通能力，要懂得如何把知识传授给学生，要了解怎样管理班级，要乐于同年轻人打交道。

想成为历史教师，学生需要在高中就开始掌握所需的技能。他们要修社会研究课程，要能辅导同学，能和小孩打交道。进行社会研究并学会如何与其他人打交道可以为他们的大学研究做准备。

要教授历史，必须在这个领域获得学十学位。历史教师需要修完美国

---

degree *n.* （大学）学位

gain *v.* 获得；取得

present *v.* 表达；介绍

tutor *v.* 教；指导

the field. They complete courses in U.S. and world history. They learn about *diverse* peoples and ways of life. They may study foreign languages as well.

While in college, some students join teacher-training programs. They take classes in teaching methods. Such courses help new teachers learn to work with students. In their last year of college, students in teaching programs act as student teachers. They work in junior high or high school classrooms. *Skilled* history teachers observe them and help them.

More and more, those who wish to be teachers work toward *advanced* degrees after college. Many earn master's degrees. *Master*'s programs often take two years. These degrees open the doors to better jobs.

历史和世界历史的课程，需要了解不同的人及其生活方式，同时也要学习外语。

在大学期间，有些学生参加教师培训项目。这些学生要修教学法课程，这些课程帮助新老师学会如何与学生合作。大学的最后一年里，参加培训项目的学生在初高中任实习教师。经验丰富的历史教师对他们进行指导。

越来越多想做教师的学生在本科毕业后致力于获得更高的学位。很多人获得了硕士学位。硕士课程通常为两年。有了硕士学位，他们就可以有机会找到更好的工作。

---

diverse *adj.* 不同的；多种多样的
advanced *adj.* 高级的；高等的

skilled *adj.* 有技能的；熟练的
master *n.* 硕士；有硕士学位的人

Once trained, a teacher must *obtain* a license or a certificate. States usually require teachers to pass one or more exams before they get their licenses.

A new teacher can find a job in many ways. Schools often recruit teachers. They *post* job ads at teacher-training schools. They also use job sites on the World Wide Web. Once a teacher *applies for* a job, the school asks for an interview. If this meeting goes well, the school may make a *job offer*. In this way, a history teacher secures a job in the classroom.

一旦接受培训，教师必须获得执照或证书。教师在取得资格证之前需要通过一门或几门考试。

新老师可以通过许多渠道找到工作。学校经常招聘教师。他们在教师培训学校张贴招聘广告，也使用万维网上的就业网站。教师在提交申请后，学校将进行面试，如果面试进行得顺利，学校会发出录用通知。这样，一份历史教师的工作就找到了。

obtain *v.* （尤指经努力）获得

apply for 申请；请求

post *v.* 发布；张贴

job offer 工作机会

34

Resolving Conflict: A Social Studies Lesson

Ivan borrowed a library book from Nick. He finished reading it. Then he left the book in the basket on Nick's bike without telling Nick. The next day Nick asked Ivan to return the book. Ivan told Nick that he had returned the book. But the book was *gone*. Nick was angry. He felt that Ivan should help him pay for the library book. Ivan did not agree.

解决冲突：社会研究的一课

伊万从尼克那里借了一本图书馆的藏书。他读完了这本书，然后在没有告知尼克的情况下把书放在了尼克自行车的车筐中。第二天，尼克向伊万要这本书，伊万说已把书还给他了。但是，书不见了。尼克很生气，他觉得伊万应该赔偿这本书，伊万不同意。

---

gone *adj.* 不复存在；丢失的

Ms. Chen noticed Nick's anger. She *took* him *aside* to talk about the problem. Then she asked Nick and Ivan to discuss their conflict in social studies class. They agreed.

Ms. Chen explained the day's lesson to the class. They were going to learn about resolving conflicts. Without taking sides, the class would help the two students work out their differences. Ms. Chen asked Nick and Ivan to tell their stories. The class then asked questions. Nick and Ivan worked together to define their problem. Ms. Chen asked them to *identify* solutions. The class added ideas to the list of solutions. Soon, Nick and Ivan agreed to a *resolution*. They would share the cost of the lost book. They signed an agreement and shook hands. Nick did not feel angry anymore. He felt that, with the help of the class, he and Ivan had reached an *equitable* solution.

陈老师看到尼克很生气，她把尼克叫到一旁询问此事。她建议尼克和伊万可以在社会研究课上讨论这个问题，他们同意了。

陈老师在课堂上讲解了当天的课程。他们将要学习如何解决矛盾。在不偏袒任何一方的情况下，同学们帮助尼克和伊万解决分歧。陈老师要求尼克和伊万讲出他们的故事，然后全班同学进行了提问，尼克和伊万共同认清了问题，陈老师要求他们对解决办法达成共识，全班同学为此出谋划策。很快，两人就解决办法达成一致，他们共同承担书费，他们签订了协议，并握手言和。尼克也不再生气了，他觉得在同学们的帮助下他和伊万找到了一个公正的解决办法。

---

take aside 把……叫到一旁
resolution *n.* 决议；解决

identify *v.* 确定；确认
equitable *adj.* 公正的；公平合理的

35

East Meets West on the Silk Road

Imagine a *relay race*. An athlete holding a *baton* runs a certain distance. Then he passes it to the next runner. That person runs on farther and then passes the baton to a third runner. Now imagine that the runners are not passing a baton. They are passing silk, gold, spices, fruit, and glass. Imagine that the race does not move

丝绸之路上东西方的融合

想象一场接力赛：一位运动员手持接力棒跑完一段距离后，将接力棒传给第二位运动员，第二位运动员再向前跑一段距离后，将接力棒传给第三位运动员。再想象一下，运动员们传接的不是接力棒，

---

relay race 接力赛   baton *n.* （接力赛的）接力棒

forward in just one direction. Instead, each runner goes *back and forth* along a path, trading goods at each end of his route. Now suppose that the runners are merchants leading caravans of camels. They earn their living by traveling the ancient Silk Road.

The Silk Road was a complex trading *network*. It passed through thousands of cities and towns. It stretched from eastern China, across Central Asia and the Middle East, to the Mediterranean Sea. It was used from about 200 b.c. to about a.d. 1300, when sea travel offered new routes. It was sometimes called the world's longest *highway*. However, the Silk Road was a series of routes, not one smooth path. The routes crossed mountains and skirted deserts. They passed through what are now 18 countries. The Silk Road had many dangers. These dangers ranged from *scorching* sun and deep

---

而是丝绸、黄金、香料、水果和琉璃。现在想象一下，比赛不是单向赛跑，而是沿着一条路线往返，在终点交换商品。现在假设运动员们都是商人，他们带领骆驼商队在丝绸之路上赚钱谋生。

丝绸之路是一张复杂的贸易网。它途经数千座城镇，从东方的中国延伸至中亚和中东地区直至地中海地区。丝绸之路起源于大约公元前200年，一直到公元1300年，因海运新航线的出现才结束，它有时被称为世界上最长的交通路线。但是丝绸之路不是一条平坦之路，它由许多路线集合而成，穿过崎岖的高山和偏远的沙漠，途经现在的18个国家。丝绸之路沿途危险重重，有烈日和暴雪，也有匪徒和战争，只有熟知这里的商人才

---

back and forth 反复来回
highway *n.* 公路；交通要道

network *n.* 网络；网状系统
scorching *adj.* 酷热的；猛烈的

snow to *bandits* and battles. Only expert traders could survive.

The Silk Road got its name from its most prized product. Silk could be used like money to pay taxes or buy goods. But the traders carried more than just silk. Gold, silver, and glass from Europe were much sought after in the Middle East and Asia. Horses traded from the *steppe* region changed farming and military practices in China and other regions. Indian merchants traded salt, spices, and precious *gems*. Chinese merchants traded porcelain and medicine. They also traded paper, which quickly replaced *parchment* in the West. Apples traveled from central Asia to Rome. The Chinese had learned to graft different trees together to make new kinds of fruit. They passed this science on to others, including the Romans. The Romans used grafting to domesticate the apple. Trading along the

---

能逃过这些灾难。

　　丝绸之路因其最珍贵的物品——丝绸——而得名，丝绸可以充当货币用来缴税和购买商品。但是在丝绸之路上，商人们交易的不仅仅是丝绸：欧洲的金银和琉璃制品在中东和亚洲地区很受欢迎；草原地区的商人用马匹交换中国或其他地区的农产品和军火；印度商人交易盐巴、香料和贵重的宝石；中国商人交易瓷器和药材，他们也交易纸张，很快这种纸张在西方代替了羊皮纸；苹果从中亚地区卖到罗马，中国人学会用不同树木嫁接出新品种水果，后来此技术传播到包括罗马在内的其他地区，罗马人通过

---

bandit *n.* 土匪

gem *n.* （经切割打磨的）宝石

steppe *n.* 草原；干草原

parchment *n.* 羊皮纸

Silk Road led to widespread *global commerce* 2,000 years before the World Wide Web.

The people along the Silk Road did not share just goods. They also shared their beliefs. *Monks*, priests, and others taught people along the Silk Road about their religions. The Silk Road created pathways for learning, *diplomacy*, and religion.

嫁接技术得到了苹果。丝绸之路早在万维网出现2 000年前就促进了国际贸易。

丝绸之路上的商人不仅买卖商品，他们还传播自己的信仰。传教士、僧侣和其他宗教信徒在丝绸之路上向人们布道。因此，丝绸之路为各国间的相互学习、外交和宗教传播创造了一个平台。

---

global *adj.* 全球的；全世界的

monk *n.* 僧侣；传教士

commerce *n.* 贸易；商务

diplomacy *n.* 外交

36

What Is Silk and How Is It Made?

Legend has it that a Chinese empress found the secrets of silk 5,000 years ago. The empress was walking by a *mulberry* tree. All at once, a *silkworm*'s *cocoon* fell into her tea and *unwound*. For thousands of years, China safeguarded the secrets of silk. It was the only place in the world to find this warm,

丝绸和丝绸的由来

传说在5 000年前，一位中国皇后发现了丝绸的秘密。当时皇后在桑树边散步，突然一个蚕茧掉入了她的热茶中渐渐散开。千百年来，中国一直保护着蚕丝的奥秘。世界上只有这里能找到这种温暖、轻薄、奢华的纺织物。随着丝绸之路的开辟，贸易往来日渐频繁，丝

---

mulberry *n.* 桑树
cocoon *n.* 茧；防护层

silkworm *n.* 蚕
unwind *v.* 解开；打开；松开

lightweight, *lavish* fabric. After trading began along the Silk Road, the secret spread to other countries.

Silk comes from the cocoon of the silkworm *moth*. A *caterpillar* hatches from the moth's egg. It spends nearly a month eating mulberry leaves. It will eat nothing else. Then it *spins* a cocoon. This takes about three days. To make the cocoon, the silkworm secretes, or gives off, two substances from its head. The first is a liquid protein. This hardens in the air into silk fiber. The second is a sticky jelly. The jelly holds the fiber in place. The caterpillar winds the fiber around itself into a tight case.

The cocoon is dropped into hot water so the jelly will melt. When the fiber loosens, it can be unwound. Each cocoon is made of one fiber more than a mile long. Five to ten fibers must be spun together to make a thread of silk. Silk thread can be used for weaving, knitting, or sewing.

绸之奥秘也传播到了其他国家。

　　丝绸来自蚕茧，蚕是由飞蛾卵孵化而来的。蚕需要进食近一个月的桑叶，其他任何食物都不吃，随后蚕开始作茧，这个过程需要三天的时间。为了作茧，蚕从头部分泌出两种物质，第一种是液化蛋白质，在空中变硬形成丝纤维。第二种是一种黏性胶状物，这种黏性物使纤维胶合在一起。毛虫利用纤维缠绕的方式使自己进入了一个密闭的环境里。

　　把茧放到热水中使这种胶状物质溶化，当纤维松散后，茧就会破展开，每只茧都是由长度大于一米的纤维构成的。一根丝线必须由五至十根纤维同时旋织而成。丝线可用来编织、针织和缝纫。

---

lavish *adj.* 大量的；奢侈的

caterpillar *n.* 毛虫；蠋

moth *n.* 蛾；飞蛾

spin *v.* 吐（丝）；作（茧）

37

Symbols of Patriotism

Symbols help unite a group or a country. Three important symbols of the United States are the *Liberty* Bell, the *bald eagle*, and the Statue of Liberty.

The Liberty Bell is a symbol of freedom. The first bell was cast in London in 1752. It had been ordered by the Pennsylvania Assembly for its State House. The bell

爱国主义的象征

象征使某一群体或者一个国家更加团结。美国的三个重要的象征是自由钟、白头鹰和自由女神。

自由钟是自由的象征。1752年，第一座钟在伦敦铸成，它是宾夕法尼亚州议会为州议会大楼定购的。1753年，这座钟悬挂于费城。第一次

---

liberty *n.* 自由   bald eagle 白头雕；白头鹫

was hung in Philadelphia in 1753. The first time it was rung to test its sound, it *cracked*. Two workers cast a new bell. They used the metal from the British bell. This bell rang only for special events. It rang on July 8, 1776, at the first public reading of *the Declaration of Independence*. The last time the bell rang was in 1846, when it rang for George Washington's birthday. The bell cracked, creating the *zigzag fracture* it still has today. The bell is on display in Philadelphia.

The bald eagle is our national *emblem*. It was chosen in 1782. The eagle lives on top of a mountain. It has unlimited freedom in its flight. This made it a good choice for a new nation focused on freedom and liberty. The bald eagle has a long life. It can live for more than 30 years in the wild. This made it a great symbol for the long life the founders hoped America would enjoy. The eagle appears on the Great Seal of the United States and on other patriotic items, such as

---

为检验声音而敲响之时，居然破裂了。两名工人又铸造了一座新钟，以那座英国钟做材料，只有在特殊时刻才敲响这座钟。1776年7月8日，第一次对公众宣读《独立宣言》时响起了它的声音。人们最后一次听到钟声是在1846年，当时是为了庆祝乔治·华盛顿的生日，然而钟又破裂了，裂开的锯齿形裂缝保留至今。目前，自由钟在费城展出。

白头鹰是美国的国徽，在1782年选定。白头鹰生活在高山的山顶，能够自由地翱翔。对于一个崇尚自由和解放的新国家来说，它成了很好的选择。白头鹰寿命很长，在野外能生存30年以上，对于当时希望美国可以长久兴旺的开国者们来说，它成了极好的象征。在美国官方大纹章上和诸

---

crack *v.* 破裂；裂开
fracture *n.* 断裂；破裂

zigzag *n.* 锯尺形线条（或形状）
emblem *n.* 徽章；标记

state flags.

The Statue of Liberty is a much newer symbol of the nation. The statue is located in New York. It was a gift from the people of France. They raised the money for the statue. They hoped to have it ready by 1876. They wanted to honor the United States on its 100th birthday. But they did not have enough money to complete it until 1886. The designer broke the statue down into 350 pieces to ship it to New York by boat. Once it arrived, crews took four months to rebuild it. The people of the United States helped create this symbol too. They raised the money to build the *pedestal*. The statue measures 305 feet from the ground to the tip of the *torch*. There are seven *rays* in the statue's crown. These rays stand for the seven seas and the seven *continents*. The Statue of Liberty stands as a symbol of freedom to people around the world.

如美国国旗等爱国主义物品上都有白头鹰。

　　自由女神像是美国比较新的一个象征。这座雕像坐落在纽约，是法国人民的礼物。法国人曾为它筹钱，想在美国建国100周年时表达敬意，所以希望1876年之前雕像能够竣工。但是直到1886年，他们才筹到足够的钱完成自由女神像的建造。设计者把雕像拆分成了350个部件，用船运到纽约。到岸后，船上工作人员花费了四个月时间把它重新安装起来。当然，美国人民也在自由女神像建造中付出了不少努力，他们筹钱建成了底座。从地面到火炬顶部，雕像高305英尺。女神的王冠上有七道尖芒，代表着世界七大洲和七大洋。对全世界人民来说，自由女神像也是自由的象征。

---

pedestal *n.* 底座；基座
ray *n.* 光线；射线

torch *n.* 火炬；火把
continent *n.* 大陆；洲

38

Betsy Ross and the American Flag

Most people think Betsy Ross *sewed* the first U.S. flag. But recently people have begun to *question* this idea. It is known that she was one of the people who sewed an early flag. But no one is sure who sewed the very first flag. However, of those first people to sew the flag, Ross is the best known.

贝齐·罗斯和美国国旗

大多数人认为，贝齐·罗斯缝制了第一面美国国旗，但是最近人们开始对此持怀疑态度。众所周知，她是参与缝制早期国旗的成员之一。但是没有人能够确定到底谁是缝制第一面美国国旗的人。然而，当时缝制国旗的成员中，罗斯是最著名的。

---

sew *v.* 缝；缝制　　　　　　　　question *v.* 怀疑；表示疑问

Betsy Ross worked as an *upholsterer*. In those days, it was common for an upholsterer to do many kinds of sewing. This included sewing flags. George Washington and Betsy Ross knew each other. They attended the same church. Ross had sewn many items for Washington in the past. In 1776 Washington asked her to sew a flag.

Her flag is known as the Betsy Ross flag. It has 13 stripes, seven red and six white. The stripes stand for the 13 colonies. The flag has 13 stars arranged in a circle. The stars represent a *constellation* in the night sky. This is a group of stars in the night sky. This design shows equality. No colony had more power than another. No one knows what happened to the first flag. Very few flags survive from that time.

The flag design changed as more states joined the nation. Now the flag has 50 stars, one for each state.

贝齐·罗斯是一名家具饰品商。那个时候，家具饰品商提供多种缝制服务是很常见的。缝制旗帜就是其中之一。乔治·华盛顿和贝齐·罗斯相识，他们在同一个教堂做礼拜。罗斯曾为华盛顿缝制过很多东西。1776年，华盛顿请她缝制一面国旗。

她缝制的国旗叫做贝齐·罗斯旗。旗上共有13道条纹，七道红色，六道白色。这些条纹代表13个殖民地。国旗上另有13颗星呈环形排列，这些星星代表夜空中的星座，也就是在夜空中的一组群星。这样的设计表达了平等的概念，即没有任何一个殖民地的权力高于其他殖民地。无人知晓关于第一面国旗的故事。那个时期的国旗几乎都没有保留下来。

随着更多的州的加入，国旗的设计也发生了变化。现在美国国旗有50颗星星，每颗星代表一个州。

---

upholsterer *n.* 家具装饰商   constellation *n.* 星座

39

Henry Ford and the First Assembly Line

In 1913 Henry Ford built the first *conveyor-belt assembly* line. It was in his Model T car factory. He started with an assembly line for just one part of the car. It had taken 20 minutes to make that one part. With the assembly line, it took only 5 minutes. So he put in more assembly lines. They cut the time needed to make a car

亨利·福特和第一条装配线

1913年，亨利·福特在他的T型汽车工厂建成了第一条传送带式装配线。他创建这条装配线只是为了汽车的一个零件。以往制造这个零件需要20分钟，然而在装配线上仅需5分钟。于是，他增加了更多的装配线。这样制造一辆小轿车的时间从17个小时缩减到了93分钟。

---

conveyor-belt *adj.* 传送带的   assembly *n.* 装配；组装

from 17 hours to just 93 minutes.

Ford's assembly line combined three key ideas. The first idea was breaking a big job into smaller tasks. This had been done in the *textile* industry. One person used to do all the tasks needed to turn cotton into cloth. However, in the 1700s, factories divided the work into smaller tasks. One group would just spin cotton. Another group would *thread* the *loom*. By breaking the work into smaller tasks, workers specialized in one part of making cloth.

The second idea made sure that work flowed at a smooth pace. All the things needed to perform a task were ready at the right time. No time was wasted. In the 1800s, *meatpackers* in Chicago had found a way to make work flow evenly. They built a machine that could

---

福特的装配线组合了三个重要理念。第一个理念就是把一项大型的作业任务分解成若干较小的作业。这个理念其实已经应用于纺织业中。过去，把棉花制成布料所需要的全部作业都由一个人完成，然而，在18世纪，工厂把这份作业分成若干的小任务。一组人员只负责纺棉花，而另一组人员负责用织布机织出布料。通过细化作业，不同的工人专门从事制作布料工艺的某一部分。

第二个重要理念就是生产流程的顺畅。执行任务所需的一切都要在恰当的时间准备好，一分一秒也不能浪费。19世纪时，芝加哥肉类加工者就找到了保持流程均衡的方法。他们制造了一种机器，靠它可以匀速地把肉

---

textile *n.* 纺织品　　　　　　thread *v.* 把……线编织进
loom *n.* 织布机　　　　　　meatpacker *n.* 肉类企业主；肉类加工者

move meat from worker to worker at an even pace. Each worker had a station and a task. The machine brought meat to the station just long enough for the worker to do the task. The machine kept the meat moving from station to station.

The third idea was to build machines with *standardized* parts. In the past, workers made each part by hand. No two parts were exactly *alike*. *For instance*, the parts used to make a gun were very complex. It took a long time to make each part and then to fit the parts together to make a gun. In 1797 Eli Whitney found a way to make gun parts by machine. The machine could make parts quickly, and the parts were standardized.

Henry Ford was the first to put all three of these ideas together. In his Model T plant, work was broken into small tasks. Each worker

---

从一个工人传给另一个工人。每个工人都有自己的工作站和任务。机器把肉类运到指定工作站的时间正好足够让工人完成任务。这种机器把肉类不断从一个工作站传送到下一个工作站。

第三个理念就是用标准化零件制造机器。过去，工人手工制造零件，所以没有任何两个零件是一模一样的。比如说，用来制作枪的那些零件都很复杂，所以每个零件的制造都要花很长的时间，然后再花很长时间把各个零件组合起来制成枪。1797年，伊莱·惠特尼找到了用机器为枪制造零件的方法。机器可快速制造出零件，而且都是标准化零件。

亨利·福特是第一个把这三个理念融合在一起的人。在他的T型汽车

---

standardize *v.* 使标准化   alike *adj.* 相像
for instance 例如；比如

had a station and a task. The conveyor belt moved parts from station to station, stopping long enough for the workers to complete their tasks. The car parts were standardized so parts fit together easily. Ford produced Model Ts quicker and cheaper, so many *ordinary* people were able to buy them.

工厂里，作业任务都拆分成很多小作业。每个工人都有自己的工作站和作业任务。传送带把零部件从一个工作站传送到另一个工作站，停留的时间足够让工人完成他们的作业任务。标准化的汽车零部件使得各零部件很容易组装在一起。这样福特公司就能以更快的速度生产T型汽车，价格也更便宜，所以许多老百姓都有能力购买了。

---

ordinary *adj.* 普通的；平凡的

40

The Impact of Mass Production

The first cars were built in the 1890s. These cars were made by hand, piece by piece. The car makers—or the buyers—could ask for any details they wanted. But the cars cost a lot and took a long time to make. Henry Ford wanted to make cars people could *afford*. He used standardized parts and a conveyor-belt

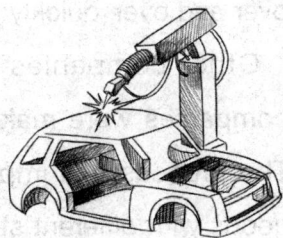

大批量生产的冲击

19世纪九十年代世界上首批轿车问世。这批汽车都是手工制造，由一个个零件组装而成的。无论是汽车制造商，还是购买者都可以有细节上的特殊要求。但是这些车造价昂贵，制造时间很长。亨利·福特希望汽车成为人们买得起的商品。于是，他采用标准零部件和传送带装配线，加快汽车的生产速度。由于福特汽车制造成本降低，很多人都能买

---

afford *v.* 买得起；能做

assembly line to make cars quickly. His cars cost less to make. Millions of people could afford them. By 1927 he had sold 15 million Model T cars.

The Model T did not have as many *options* as cars have today. In fact, it did not have any options at all. Each Model T was just like all the others. All the cars were black. They were all the same size. They all had the same parts. Using the same parts kept the assembly line moving quickly and smoothly. This method of making the same thing over and over, quickly and cheaply, is called *mass production*.

Other companies started to use this process. Soon many companies were making goods quickly that people could afford. The process has improved. Now companies can *customize* their goods with different styles and features. Cars, furniture, *dishwashers*, computers, and many other products are made today on assembly lines.

得起了。截止到1927年，他已经售出了1 500万辆T型汽车。

那时的T型汽车不像今天的汽车有那么多的附件配饰，实际上它没有任何附件配饰。所有的T型汽车一模一样，都是黑色的，尺寸一样，所用的零部件也都完全一样。采用相同的零部件使得整个生产线运行更快，更顺畅。这种快速，低成本地重复制造同一产品的方式称为大批量生产。

其他公司开始相继采用这种模式。很快，许多公司都制造出生产快速、人们买得起的商品。这个加工过程也逐步完善，现在很多公司可以定做不同风格、不同特点的商品。如今，汽车、家具、洗碗机、计算机和许多其他产品都出自于这种生产线。

---

option *n.* 可选择的事物；选择
customize *v.* 订制；定做

mass production 大批量生产
dishwasher *n.* 洗碗碟机

41

The Spanish-American War

The Spanish-American War was a short war. It was fought between the United States and Spain. The war *took place* in 1898. It *lasted* only four months. The war was fought on two fronts. Some of the fighting took place in Cuba. Cuba is a country in the Caribbean Sea. Some of the fighting took place in the Philippines. These

美西战争

美西战争是一场耗时不长的战争,仅仅持续了四个月。交战双方是美国和西班牙。这场战争发生在1898年,战事在两条战线上展开。一些战役在加勒比海国家——古巴打响,另外一些激战发生在太平

---

take place 发生　　　　　　　　　　　　　　　last *v.* 持续;继续

islands are in the Pacific Ocean.

The Spanish Empire was once very powerful. Since 1492 Spain had been sending explorers around the world. Cuba and the Philippines both belonged to Spain. Spain treated both countries *harshly*. The people of both countries wanted freedom from Spain's control. People in the United States sympathized with them. But the United States was not ready to go to war with Spain.

Two *key* events brought the United States and Spain to war. The first was a letter published in the *New York Journal*. This letter was stolen from the Spanish *minister* in Washington. The letter said bad things about President McKinley. It made people think that Spain was making fun of the United States. A few months later the U.S.S. Maine, an American *battleship*, blew up in a Cuban harbor. Two

---

洋上的菲律宾群岛。

　　西班牙帝国曾经雄霸一时。自1492年起，西班牙的探险家们就已遍布全世界。古巴和菲律宾同为西班牙的殖属地。西班牙长期残酷的殖民统治，令两国人民极力想要摆脱其统治获得自由。尽管美国人对古巴和菲律宾人民表示同情，但是美国还没做好准备与西班牙进行交战。

　　两起关键事件引发了美国对西班牙的战争。第一件是公开发表在《纽约杂志》上的一封信。这封信是从驻华盛顿的西班牙部长那里偷来的。信上说了美国麦金莱总统的坏话，这让人们认为西班牙在取笑美国。几个月后，美国军舰"缅因"号———艘美国战舰，在古巴港爆炸，造成260人

---

harshly *adv.* 残酷地；严酷地　　　　　　key *adj.* 主要的；关键的

minister *n.* 部长；大臣　　　　　　　　battleship *n.* 战舰；战列舰

hundred sixty men died. Many people thought Spain had bombed the ship. However, that was not proved. In March 1898, *Senator* Redfield Proctor spoke to the Senate about Spain's cruel treatment of the Cuban people. McKinley told Spain to leave Cuba. Five days later the United States *declared* war on Spain.

Before these events, the United States had wanted to buy Cuba. Cuba had a large sugar cane industry. The United States thought this was very valuable. The United States had *invested* a great deal of money in Cuba. Spain's harsh treatment of Cuba had harmed U.S. business interests.

The war was the subject of much debate in the United States. Many people felt the United States was being too *aggressive*. They felt the United States should not try to take new lands. Others

---

死亡。许多人认为西班牙轰炸了这艘战舰。然而，此事并没有得到任何证实。1898年3月，参议员雷德菲尔德·普罗科特对参议院陈述了西班牙对古巴人民的残酷统治。美国总统麦金莱责令西班牙撤出古巴。五天之后，美国对西班牙宣战。

这些事件之前，美国曾希望购买古巴。古巴有很大的甘蔗工业，这是美国认为非常有价值的产业。美国已经在古巴投入了大量资金。西班牙对古巴的严苛殖民统治已经伤害到了美国的商业利益。

战争，在美国是备受争议的话题。很多人认为美国过于好战，认为美国不应该再去占有新的领土。还有人认为，这个国家有义务在整个世界传

---

senator *n.* 参议员　　　　　　　　declare *v.* 宣布；宣告
invest *v.* 投资；投入　　　　　　aggressive *adj.* 好斗的；侵略性的

thought the country had a duty to spread its way of life throughout the world. This way of thinking is called *manifest destiny*.

The Spanish-American War increased U.S. land *holdings*. *The Treaty of Paris*, signed in France in 1898, ended the war. Cuba gained its *independence* from Spain. The United States now owned Guam, Puerto Rico, and the Philippine Islands. This victory *established* the United States as a world power.

播它的生活方式，这种思维方式被称为"天定命运论"。

美西战争增加了美国的土地储备。1898年，《巴黎条约》在法国签署，战争结束。古巴脱离了西班牙的统治获得了独立。美国现在拥有关岛、波多黎各和菲律宾群岛。这一胜利为美国成为世界强国奠定了基础。

---

manifest destiny 宿命；天定命运论   holding *n.* 私有财产；所有物

independence *n.* 独立；自主   establish *v.* 建立；确立

42

Puerto Rico Becomes a United States Territory

Puerto Rico once *belonged to* Spain. But Puerto Rico has had a troubled history. It has long sought freedom. In 1897 Spain gave Puerto Rico some freedom. But this freedom did not last long.

In 1898 the United States and Spain fought each other in the Spanish-American War. The war lasted four months. Spain

波多黎各

波多黎各曾经是西班牙的殖民地，不过它有段混乱的历史。波多黎各长期寻求自由。1879年，西班牙曾给它一些自由，但持续的时间并不长。

1898年，美国和西班牙之间爆发了美西战争。战争持续了四个月，

---

belong to 属于；归……所有

surrendered. The United States gained control of Puerto Rico. This meant the country belonged to the United States. Both the United States and Spain signed *the Treaty of Paris in France*. The *treaty* made the exchange official.

The United States kept Puerto Rico under military rule until 1900. In 1917 the United States gave the Puerto Rican people U.S. citizenship. In 1952 Puerto Ricans gained the right to elect their own officials. However, Puerto Rico still does not have a representative in the U.S. Congress. Its people cannot vote for the U.S. president. They do not pay *federal* income taxes.

Puerto Rico's standard of living has improved. Most people can read. Roads are in good shape. People are healthier. The United States has also benefited from the *alliance*. Puerto Rico is a good

---

最终以西班牙的投降而告终。美国因此取得了对波多黎各的统治权，波多黎各沦为美国的殖民地。美国和西班牙在法国签署了《巴黎条约》，条约中注明了正式的殖民地归属权变更事宜。

直到1900年波多黎各一直处于美国的军事统治下。1917年，美国给予波多黎各人美国公民身份。1952年，波多黎各人获得选举自己政府官员的权利。然而，波多黎各在美国国会仍然没有一个代表。波多黎各人不能投票选举美国总统，也不用支付联邦所得税。

如今，波多黎各人的生活水平得到了改善。多数人能认字，人民身体更加健康；道路状况也良好。美国也受益于这种联盟。波多黎各成为了美

---

surrender *v.* 投降
federal *adj.* 联邦制的；联邦政府的

treaty *n.* 条约；协定
alliance *n.* 联盟；同盟

naval base for the United States.

People still discuss Puerto Rico's future. Should it become a state? Should it claim independence? Or should it remain a U.S. *territory*?

国的一个优良的海军基地。

人们仍然会谈论波多黎各的未来。它应该成为美国的一个州吗？它应该宣布独立吗？还是应该继续作为隶属于美国疆土的一部分呢？

---

naval *adj.* 海军的   base *n.* 基地
territory *n.* 领土；版图

43

The Planning of Washington, D.C.

After the Revolutionary War, the United States became a new nation. As a nation, it needed a capital. Planning the city was a *major* task. The city had to be grand. It had to be a symbol to the world.

In 1790 George Washington chose the *site* for the capital. It was on the banks of

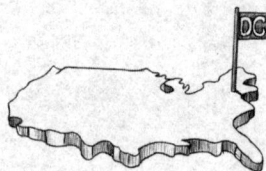

华盛顿特区的规划

独立战争后，美国变成了一个新的国家。作为一个国家，它需要一个首都。都市规划是一项重大的工作。首都一定要宏伟壮观，因为对世界来说它是一个国家的象征。

1790年，乔治·华盛顿为首都选址。地点位于波多马克河岸，地处

---

major *adj.* 主要的；重要的   site *n.* 地点；位置

the Potomac River. It was in the center of the 13 states. It was also near the Atlantic coast. The city needed to be near the ocean so that it would be easy to trade with Europe.

The next step was to choose a designer for the city. Washington chose Pierre L'Enfant. L'Enfant was a French engineer. He loved the new country. He wrote to Washington and asked if he could be the city designer. In 1791 he finished the design. But he did not finish the project. He had a bad *temper*, so Washington *fired* him. L'Enfant took his plans with him when he left. Benjamin Banneker, an African American who was part of the design team, redrew the plans from memory. In 1792 crews laid the *cornerstone* for the White House.

L'Enfant's city plan was a *diamond* measuring 10 miles on each side. The city would have wide streets linking points of interest. The

---

13个州的中心，也临近大西洋海岸。首都临近大海，可以为与欧洲进行贸易提供便利条件。

下一步是选一位设计师。华盛顿选择了皮埃尔·朗方，一位法国工程师。皮埃尔·朗方喜欢这个新国家，便写信给华盛顿，问他是否可以成为首都设计师。1791年，他完成了设计，遗憾的是他没能完成这个项目。因为他脾气很坏，所以华盛顿解雇了他，于是他带着他的设计离开了。设计团队的一员——非裔美国人本杰明·班纳克，根据记忆重画了规划图。1792年，设计组铺下了白宫的基石。

皮埃尔·朗方把城市规划成一个边长为10英里的菱形。宽阔的街道

---

temper *n.* 脾气；情绪　　　　　　　　fire *v.* 解雇；开除
cornerstone *n.* 基石；奠基石　　　　diamond *n.* 菱形

avenues in the city were set in *diagonals*. They *branched out* from the two main buildings in the city: the Capitol and the White House. L'Enfant used lots of open space in his plan. He wanted to connect with the natural *landscape* as much as he could. He thought a city should use its natural resources in its design.

In 1902 the city went through one more major change. Senator James McMillan put together a new design group. He wanted the group to design a large park system for the city. Group members looked back at the L'Enfant plan while doing their own work. They went to Europe for seven weeks. They were told to study the great capitals of Europe. McMillan wanted a European *influence* for the U.S. capital.

连接城中的重要地点。按照对角线来修建城市的街道。街道以两个主要的城市建筑即国会大厦及白宫为中心向外分散。朗方在他的设计规划中使用大量的开放空间。他想尽可能地运用自然景观，因为他认为一个城市的设计应该充分利用其自然资源。

1902年，这座城市经历了一次巨变。参议员詹姆斯·麦克米伦组建了一个新的设计团队。他希望设计一个大型的城市公园体系。设计团队成员做设计时也回顾了朗方的设计方案。麦克米伦希望美国首都具有欧洲的风格，他要求设计团队研究欧洲各国的雄伟首都，因此设计团队去欧洲考察了七个星期。

---

diagonal *n.* 对角线；斜线　　　　　　　　branch out 扩展范围
landscape *n.* 风景；景色　　　　　　　　influence *n.* 影响；作用

The *committee* members made big plans for the city. They created a complete park system. They chose sites for government buildings. They improved the Mall area and cleaned up the city. As time went on, the city added more museums and monuments. Together, two great plans helped create the city that visitors now see.

该委员会成员为首都做了伟大的规划。他们创造了一个完整的公园系统，为政府大楼选址，改进城市的购物中心并且清理了城市。随着时间的推移，这个城市增加了更多的博物馆和纪念碑。两个伟大的城市规划共同创建了现在游客眼中的城市。

committee *n.* 委员会

44

The Lincoln Memorial

The Lincoln Memorial is located in Washington, D.C. It is a *tribute* to Abraham Lincoln. He was the sixteenth president of the United States. During the Civil War, Lincoln had helped keep the Union strong. But he was killed in 1865, just days after the war ended. The structure was built to *honor* Lincoln's work during

林肯纪念馆

林肯纪念馆位于华盛顿特区，它表达了人们对亚伯拉罕·林肯——第十六任美国总统的敬意。在内战期间，林肯维护了联邦政府的强大。但1865年，在内战结束仅仅几天后，林肯就遇害了。这个建筑用来纪念林肯在内战期间所作出的贡献。1914年，纪念馆开始施工修建，于1922年完工。

tribute *n.* 致敬；颂词   honor *v.* 尊敬；给予荣誉

the Civil War. In 1914 work began on the *memorial*. It was finished in 1922.

The building looks like a Greek temple. It has 36 columns. Each column stands for one of the 36 states that were part of the union when Lincoln was president. The building contains stones from many states. The outside is made of marble from Colorado. *Limestone* from Indiana is on the inside walls. Pink marble from Tennessee is on the floor. Marble from Alabama is on the ceiling.

Many *inscriptions* are on the walls. The Gettysburg Address is on the south wall. There is also a *mural* on that wall. It shows the angel of truth freeing an enslaved person. All these things have to do with ideas that Lincoln cherished. The statue of Lincoln is in the center of the building. It is 19 feet tall and 19 feet wide. It is made of 28 blocks of marble. The statue faces a long pool of water.

这座建筑看起来像一座希腊神庙。它有36根立柱，每一根立柱代表一个州，也就是林肯总统任职时，组成联邦的36个州中的一个。建筑材料中所使用的石头来自许多州：纪念馆外部的大理石来自科罗拉多州；室内墙壁的石灰石来自印第安纳州；地面的粉红色大理石来自田纳西州；天花板上的大理石则来自阿拉巴马州。

墙上有许多题词，在南墙上提有葛底斯堡演说。这面墙上还有一幅壁画，表现的是真理天使在释放被奴役的人们。所有这一切都和林肯珍视的思想有关。林肯雕像矗立在建筑物的中心。雕像19英尺高，19英尺宽，由28块大理石组成。雕像的对面有一个长长的水池。

---

memorial *n.* 纪念碑；纪念物
inscription *n.* 题词；刻写的文字

limestone *n.* 石灰岩
mural *n.* 壁画

45

The Mound Builders

Many people lived in the United States before the settlers came from Europe. These ancient peoples had complex cultures. One *trait* of these cultures was their strong tie to the land. The people used the land for many things. One thing people did with the land was create *mounds*. Scientists have found mounds built

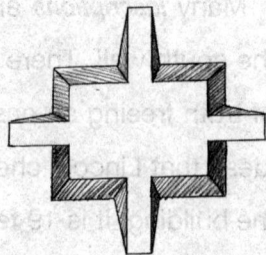

土墩建造者

来自欧洲的移居者到达美国之前，这片土地上就已有许多居民。这些古老的民族有着复杂的文化，一个显著的特点就是它们和土地有着密不可分的关系。人们依靠土地做很多事情，其中之一就是在土地上建造土墩。科学家们已经发现了许多不同族群的土著人建造的土墩，

---

trait *n.* 特征；特点   mound *n.* 土墩；小丘

by many different groups of native people. They called the people who built these mounds "Mound Builders".

Three cultures seem to have built most of the mounds found in the United States. These cultures are the Adena, the Hopewell, and the Mississippian. Each culture *contains* many groups. Of the three, the Adena culture is the oldest. It was *located* mainly in Ohio. The mounds from this culture *date back* to 1000 b.c. The Hopewell culture rose as the Adena culture was dying. The Hopewell moved as far south as Florida. This culture seemed more *informal*. The groups worked with one another as trading partners. This culture lasted about 700 years. The most recent and most advanced culture is the Mississippian. This culture had a complex religious and social structure.

Mounds can be found in many parts of the country—from New

他们称那些建造了这些土墩的人为"土墩建造者"。

在美国发现的大部分土墩似乎和三种文化有关，分别是阿登纳文化、霍普韦尔文化和密西西比文化。每种文化涵盖许多族群。三种文化中，阿登纳文化历史最悠久，主要位于俄亥俄州内。源自这一文化的土墩可以追溯到公元前1000年。在阿登纳文化行将没落的时候，霍普韦尔文化兴起。霍普韦尔文化南部远至佛罗里达。此种文化似乎更随意和不拘礼节，部落与部落之间视彼此为贸易伙伴，这一文化持续了大约700年。最近的和最先进的文化是密西西比文化，有复杂的宗教和社会结构。

美国的很多地方都可以找到土墩——从纽约到佛罗里达州，西边远至

---

contain *n.* 包含；容纳
date back 追溯到；始于

locate *v.* 位于；坐落在
informal *adj.* 友好随便的；不拘礼节的

York to Florida. They are found as far west as Nebraska. No one knows for sure just why the mounds were built.

There appear to be three main types of mounds. They are the temple mounds, the *burial* mounds, and the *effigy* mounds. The temple mounds are the oldest mounds. People may have built temples or places of *worship* on top of the mounds. People would climb *ramps* to reach the temple for worship. Some mounds had the homes of leaders built on top of them. Other mounds were burial mounds. The burial mounds were most likely built to honor the dead. Scientists have found skeletons and jewelry in some of these mounds. Effigy mounds are mounds shaped like animals, such as serpents or birds.

Each mound took many years to build. Many people worked together. People would work from dawn to dusk. They would gather

---

内布拉斯加州也能看到土墩的踪迹。没有人确切地知道这些土墩的建造原因。

　　土墩主要分为三个类型，分别是寺庙土墩、坟墩和象形丘。最古老的是寺庙土墩，可能是人们在土墩顶上建立寺庙或者建造一些敬神的场所，然后他们爬过斜坡抵达寺庙来拜神。一些头领的住宅也建在土墩的顶部。还有些土墩是墓冢，极有可能是为纪念逝者而建的。科学家们已经在一些坟丘中发现了骨骼和珠宝。雕像土墩的造型像动物，比如蛇或鸟。

　　建造一个土墩要花很多年的时间。许多人一起干活，从黎明干到黄昏。他们会用篮子盛着泥土，然后走到修建土墩的地方，把泥土倒下来，

---

burial *n.* 埋葬；葬礼　　　　　　　　　　effigy *n.* 雕像；塑像
worship *n.* 崇拜；礼拜　　　　　　　　　ramp *n.* 斜坡；坡道

baskets of dirt. Then they would go to the place where the mound was to be built and *dump* the dirt. They would *stamp* the dirt down with their feet. Then they would *gather* more dirt. This would go on day after day until a shape *emerged*. Mound building probably went on for about 5,500 years in North America.

用脚把泥土踩实，之后再去收更多的泥土。这样日复一日地重复，直到土墩成形。在北美，土墩建造大约持续了5 500年之久。

---

dump *v.* 扔掉；倾倒   stamp *v.* 重踩；重踏

gather *v.* 收集；收拢   emerge *v.* 出现；显现

46

A Visit to Effigy Mounds National Monument

Effigy Mounds National Monument is located in Iowa. The park contains almost 200 mounds. The mounds have many shapes. Some of the mounds here are *cone-shaped*. These are the oldest ones. Other mounds look like long lines. There are also about 30 effigy mounds in the park. An effigy is a shape that looks like a

参观雕像古冢国家保护区

雕像古冢国家保护区位于爱荷华州。这个公园里有近200个土墩。这些土墩形状各异：一些土墩呈锥形，也最古老；其他的土墩看起来像长长的线。公园里还有大约30座象形丘。象形丘造型栩栩如生，看起来让人想到活生生的动物，比如鸟或熊。这些象形丘大小不一。

---

cone-shaped *adj.* 锥形的

living thing, such as a bird or a bear. The mounds have various sizes. One of the biggest is the Great Bear Mound. It is 137 feet long, 70 feet across, and 3.5 feet high.

Many native groups made mounds. Mounds can be found throughout the United States. The oldest mounds in Effigy Mounds National Park were built about 500 b.c. Tools and weapons have been found in the mounds. They teach scientists how the mound builders lived. They show how the people hunted and how they made their houses and clothes.

The park also has a unique natural landscape. Its environment is more diverse than the environment of any other U.S. national park. The area has forests, tallgrass prairies, wetlands, and rivers. The park is home to beavers, *muskrats*, and red-shouldered hawks. Oak and *aspen* trees are found in the park. The park became a national monument in 1949. In 1961 it became a land and wildlife *preserve*.

其中最大的是大熊丘，长137英尺，宽70英尺，高3.5英尺。

许多土著人建造了这些土墩，它们遍布整个美国。雕像古冢国家公园里最古老的土墩建于大约公元前500年。在土墩中已经发现了工具和武器，科学家们从中了解到土墩修建者是如何生活的，也了解到人们是如何狩猎、如何建造房子和如何做衣服的。

这个公园里还有一片独特的自然景观。比起其他的美国国家公园，这里的环境更具多样化。这一区域有森林、高草草原、湿地以及河流。这里是海狸、麝鼠和赤肩鸢的家。在公园里还可以看到橡树和白杨树。1949年，公园成为国家历史文物。1961年，公园成为了野生动植物保护区。

---

muskrat n. 麝鼠
preserve n. 保护区；禁猎区

aspen n. 山杨；白杨

47

Campaigning for Office

In the United States, people can obtain official government *posts* in two ways. One way is by being *appointed*. The other is by being elected. The public casts votes to elect people to key posts. People elected to federal posts include the president and members of Congress. Those elected to state posts include the governor and

竞选政府公职

在美国，人们可以通过两种途径获得官方政府职位。一种方式是任命就职，另一种途径是经由选举当选。公众投票选出主要职位的人选。人们可参选的联邦职位包括总统职位和国会议员席位，可参选的州级职位包括州长职位和州立法委员席位，可参选的地方职位包括市长职位和学校董事会的成员席位。我们称竞选职务的人为候选人。为了得到

---

post *n.* 职位；（尤指）要职

appoint *v.* 安排；确定

state *legislators*. Those elected to local posts include the mayor and members of the school board. People who compete for office are called *candidates*. To obtain these posts, they must win an election.

Candidates work hard to gain the support of the people. They run campaigns aimed at winning votes. In their campaigns, they present their views. They want the public to know what they stand for. They want to show that the concerns of the public are their concerns. They hope to convey that they are the best choice for the post.

To reach the public, candidates use varied methods. For state and local posts, they send out *pamphlets*. Campaign workers phone voters or reach them door to door. Public forums give the voters a chance to meet and talk with those running for office. The *press* aids the candidates. News programs and newspapers report on the

---

这些职位，他们必须在选举中获胜。

候选人致力于获得民众的支持。他们举行各种宣传活动，旨在赢得选票。在活动中，他们发表自己对各种事务的看法。他们希望公众了解他们拥护什么。他们想表明，公众所关注的也正是他们所关注的。他们希望传达出他们本身就是这个职位最佳人选这样的信息。

为了接近公众，候选人采用各种不同的方式。为竞选州级职位和地方职务，他们分发宣传小册子。竞选工作人员会致电选民或挨家挨户地登门拜访。公共论坛提供了选民与竞选者见面和交流的机会。媒体也会给候选者提供帮助，新闻节目和报纸会对竞选活动进行报道。一些电视台和广播

---

legislator *n.* 立法委员
pamphlet *n.* 小册子；手册

candidate *n.* 候选人；申请人
press *n.* 新闻界；出版社

campaigns. Some TV and radio stations broadcast interviews. Local campaigns last for a few months.

A campaign for president is different. Those who run for this office campaign for more than a year. They need to reach voters across the nation. Travel is important. *Rallies* in large cities gather voter support. Meetings each day with the press spread the campaign message. Debates give candidates a chance to argue their views. Campaigns of this size call for the aid of thousands of workers.

Most of those who run for president belong to a political party. Just one member of each party can run for president. Each party names its candidate. Sometimes a *preliminary* election, or a primary, helps the party make its choice. Most states hold primary elections. Voters in each state cast their *ballots* to decide who they want to be

---

电台会播放活动采访。地方竞选活动会持续几个月之久。

但是，总统竞选大不一样。总统候选人的竞选要长达一年多。他们需要到全国各地走近选民拉选票。巡游很重要，总统候选人在大城市聚集选民进行集会活动来获得选民的支持。每天召开媒体见面会来通报最新竞选活动信息。辩论活动会给候选人公开陈述各自观点和立场的机会。这种规模的竞选活动需要成千上万的工作人员辅助完成。

大多数参加总统竞选的人都隶属某一政党。每个政党只能有一名总统候选人，各政党自己提名候选人。有时，预选举或初选举会帮助政党做出选择。大多数的州都举行初选。每个州的选民投票来决定自己选谁作为他

---

campaign *n.* 运动；竞选运动
preliminary *adj.* 预备性的；初步的

rally *n.* 公共集会；群众大会
ballot *n.* 投票表决；选票

their party's candidate. Later the party *names* the *official* candidate. This person goes on to run against the candidates of other parties. The one who earns the most public support is the one who receives the most votes. In the end, it is often the best campaign that wins the election.

们的政党提名候选人。之后，政党会提名正式候选人，该候选人将继续与其他党派的候选人竞争。赢得最多民众支持的候选人会赢得最多选票。最后，通常是最棒的竞选者赢得大选。

name *v.* 任命；提名　　　　　　　　official *adj.* 正式的；官方的

48

Why Vote?

The United States is a *democracy*. The government gains its power from the people. The people elect leaders to run the nation. A democracy gives the people many rights. One of the most basic rights is the right to vote. When a person votes, he or she *asserts* the voice of the people. Voting preserves the rights and power of

为什么要投票?

美国是一个民主国家。政府从人民手中获得权力，人民选出领导人来治理国家。民主赋予人民很多权利。其中一个最基本的权利就是投票权。当一个人投票时，他或她表现的是人民的发言权。投票维护着人民的权利和权力。林登·约翰逊总统曾经说过，如果没有投票权，

---

democracy *n.* 民主政体；民主国家   **assert** *v.* 明确肯定；维护

the people. President Lyndon Johnson once said that without the right to vote, no other right would have any meaning.

People vote for many reasons. Some go to the polls to choose leaders. They vote to elect people to office. Their votes *grant* the leaders the power to rule. In this way, the people consent to be governed. Others vote to play a part in their government. They believe their ballots have an *impact* on the fate of the nation. In some elections, people cast votes to settle local issues. Often these matters affect daily life. They may vote on public transport or the building of a new school. They mark their ballots to express their views. Their votes shape the future of their towns and districts. On all levels, the right to vote grants the people the power of *self-rule*.

其他一切权利都没有意义。

　　人们投票的原因各不相同。有些人投票选择领导人，投票选举政府公职人员，他们的选票赋予领导者治理权。通过这种方式，人们同意接受管理。其他人投票来参与政府执政。他们相信自己的选票会影响国家的命运。在一些选举中，人们投票解决当地的问题争端。通常，这些问题关乎日常生活。他们可能针对公共交通或新学校的修建进行投票。他们用选票表明自己的观点。他们的选票会决定其所在城镇和街区的未来发展方向。从各方面来讲，投票权保障了人民的自治权。

---

grant *v.* 同意；准许　　　　　　　　impact *n.* 巨大影响；强大作用
self-rule *n.* 自治

49

The Six Landform Regions of Canada

The nation of Canada lies to the north of the United States. It is a land of varied natural features. *Distinct* landforms divide the nation into six regions.

The Atlantic region *spans* the eastern coast of Canada. An old mountain range makes this region hilly and rugged. Valleys run between the hills. People farm in these

加拿大的六大地形区

加拿大位于美国的北部，是一个拥有多样化自然特征的国家。不同的地貌将这个国家划分成六个地区。

大西洋地区横跨加拿大东海岸。古老的山脉使得这一地区的地貌陡峭崎岖。山谷蜿蜒于山间，人们在谷中耕作，这里的田地可以免遭从大西洋

---

distinct *adj.* 有区别的；明显的   span *v.* 贯穿；包括

valleys. The land there is sheltered from the wind of the Atlantic Ocean. Off the coast is one of the best fishing grounds in the world. It is called the Grand Banks. Here cold *currents* from the north meet warm currents from the south.

The Great Lakes and Lowlands are inland from the eastern coast. This region shares with the United States five lakes called the Great Lakes. This is the largest group of freshwater lakes in the world. Long ago flowing rivers of ice, called glaciers, covered the region. As they melted, huge lakes formed. Over time, some of these lakes *drained*. They left behind layers of rich *sediment*. This *fertile* soil is excellent for farming.

Farther west is the Canadian Shield. This is a dome of rock that covers almost half of the nation. There is little soil in this region.

吹来的风的影响。离岸不远的一片海面被称为"大浅滩",是世界上最好的渔场之一。来自北部的寒流与来自南部的暖流在此交汇。

五大湖和低地区是自东海岸以内的内陆地区。这个地区与美国共同拥有称为"五大湖"的五个湖泊。五大湖是世界上最大的淡水湖群。很久以前,流动的冰河(亦称冰川)覆盖了这一地区。冰川融化就形成了巨大的湖泊。随着时间的推移,其中一些湖泊干涸了,留下了厚厚的沉积物层。这种肥沃的沉积土壤非常适合农耕。

深入更远的西部是加拿大的地盾区。岩石构成的圆盖几乎覆盖了这个国家一半的面积。这个地区几乎没有土壤,然而,森林却屹然生长于林立

---

current *n.* 水流;潮流;气流　　　　drain *v.* 流走;流光
sediment *n.* 沉积物;沉淀物　　　　fertile *adj.* 肥沃的;富饶的

However, forests persist *amid* the rock. Grassy *bogs*, lakes, and rivers are also abundant.

In the interior of the country are the Plains. The forests of the north give way to prairies of tall grass. Farmers here grow grain crops such as wheat. Farther south, the dry climate allows for only low grasses. This area is perfect for raising cattle.

On the western coast of Canada is the Cordillera. This is a region of *stark* contrasts. Not far from the grassy plains are ice fields, glaciers, and high mountain peaks. This region lies between two mountain ranges. They are the Rocky Mountains and the Coastal Mountains. Other landforms include deep *gorges*, high plateaus, and steep coastal cliffs. Despite the harsh landscape, forests abound. People even farm in the valleys between the ranges.

的岩石之间。这里还有大量的禾草沼泽、湖泊和河流。

　　加拿大的内陆地区是平原。长满高草的大草原代替了北部的森林。这儿的农民种植像小麦这类的谷类作物。再往南走，干燥的气候仅适合低草生长。这一地区十分适合放牧。

　　科迪勒拉山脉就在加拿大的西部海岸。这个地区自然环境对比鲜明。距离青草繁茂的平原不远处就是冰原、冰川和高高的山峰。这个地区位于落基山脉和海岸山脉两座山脉之间。其他地貌还包括幽深的峡谷、高原和陡峭的海崖。尽管地形险恶，森林比比皆是，人们还是在山脉之间的山谷中耕作。

---

amid *prep.* 在……中；四周是　　　　　　　　　　bog *n.* 沼泽
stark *adj.* 明显的；鲜明的　　　　　　　　　　　gorge *n.* 峡谷

The *uppermost* part of the nation is called the North or the Tundra. This region lies in the Arctic Circle. The winters are long and dark, and the summers are short and cool. This region *borders* the icy waters of the Arctic Ocean. Except for the top layer of soil, the ground is *frozen* year round. There are no trees and little plant life. This region is unlike any other in Canada.

人们称加拿大的最高处为"北地"或"冻原"。这个地区位于北极圈内，冬季漫长黑暗，夏季短暂凉爽。冰冷的北冰洋海水围绕着它。除表层土壤外，地面整年封冻。这里没有树，也没有什么植物。这一地区和加拿大的任何其他地区都不同。

---

uppermost *adj.* 最高的；最上面的　　　　border *v.* 沿……的边；环绕
frozen *adj.* 冰封的；冻硬的

50

The Art and Sport of Ice and Snow Sculpture

Ice *carving* and snow sculpting are sports as well as arts. The Great Lakes region of the United States and Canada *hosts* contests in these sports each winter. The region is a perfect site for these events. It has long cold winters and *ample* snowfall. The *sculptures* are works of art.

Ice carving is an art. Ice sculptures range

冰雪雕刻——艺术和运动

冰雕和雪雕既是运动也是艺术。每年冬天，美国和加拿大的五大湖地区都会举行冰雪雕塑竞赛。因为冬天寒冷漫长，降雪充足，所以该地区是举办这些比赛项目的理想地点。这样的雕塑品也是艺术品。

冰雕是一门艺术。冰雕作品范围很广，上到巨大的纪念碑，下到小小的

---

carving *n.* 雕刻；雕刻品
ample *adj.* 足够的；丰裕的

host *v.* 主办；主持
sculpture *n.* 雕像；雕塑品

from *massive* monuments to small *decorations*. The artists who make them may be sculptors or chefs. But ice carving is also a sport. Contests may last for days. Teams of two or more people sculpt *blocks* of ice the size of large *suitcases*. At some contests a team works on one block of ice. At other contests, a team may create a sculpture from 25 blocks of ice.

The art of snow sculpting attracts sculptors who normally work with other materials. They enjoy working with snow because they can make massive forms in a short time. In contests, teams of three or four people sculpt one large snow block. The blocks may be the size of a small room. They may weigh 35 tons. These contests last for two to five days. Artists work day and night to finish on time. Once completed, the snow sculptures are displayed. The sculptures remain on view as long as the cold weather lasts.

装饰品。冰雕作品创作者也许是雕塑家，也许是厨师。然而，冰雕也是一项竞技运动。比赛活动可能会持续好几天。两人或多人组成一个冰雕团队，共同雕刻那些大码手提箱大小的冰块。有些比赛中，一个团队在一个冰块上雕刻。在其他一些比赛中，一个团队可能会用25个冰块来创造一个作品。

雪雕艺术通常吸引那些用其他材料来雕刻的雕塑者。他们喜欢雪雕是因为他们可以在短时间内创造出大量艺术形式。在雪雕比赛中，三或四个人组成团队来雕刻一个巨大的雪块。雪块大概有一个小房间那样大，重35吨左右。比赛一般持续二到五天。艺术家们昼夜工作，以期按时完成雕刻任务。雪雕作品完成后，便进行展出。只要寒冷的天气持续，这些雪雕作品就可以一直展示着。

---

massive *adj.* 巨大的；结实的
block *n.* 大块；立方体

decoration *n.* 装饰品；装饰图案
suitcase *n.* （旅行用的）手提箱